Which
   Way?

A GUIDE FOR NEW CHRISTIANS

*Which
Way?*

A GUIDE FOR NEW CHRISTIANS

by

John and Karen Howe

Morehouse-Barlow Co.
New York

Acknowledgments

Except where otherwise noted, Scripture quotations are from *Good News for Modern Man,* the New Testament in Today's English Version, copyright © American Bible Society 1966, 1971, and used by permission.

The Scripture quotations marked RSV are from the Revised Standard Version of the Bible, copyrighted 1946 and 1952 by the Division of Christian Education of the National Council of the Churches of Christ in the U.S.A., and used by permission.

© 1973 by Morehouse-Barlow Co.
14 East 41st St., New York, N. Y. 10017

Standard Book Number 0-8192-1135-4

Printed in the United States of America

Contents

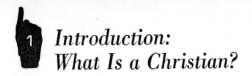

1 Introduction: What Is a Christian?

LET'S START by defining terms.

What makes someone a Christian? Does it happen when he's born into a Christian family? when he's baptized or confirmed? when he joins a church? Or, is it a matter of living a good life, being a moral person, trying to love everyone?

When we speak of "becoming a Christian," we are referring to what the New Testament calls being "saved," or being "born again." These are Biblical terms which rather graphically refer to the extraordinary experience of having God's Spirit come to live within our life when we ask him to. When Christ sends his Spirit into us, it is an event of such overwhelming significance that it can be compared only to a "new birth," a totally new beginning, the start of a life committed to God instead of selfish pursuits.

Salvation, new birth, conversion—whatever we call it—might occur in a church service but it might not. It could come at the time of baptism or confirmation, but that is not usually the case. Also, it does not seem to hinge upon the religiosity of our parents. Salvation is a highly personal experience which occurs when a seeking human heart decides to trust in God's promises and reaches out in faith for a God who responds by making himself known to that individual in an undeniable way. The new birth, the joining of human spirit with divine Spirit, cannot be programmed, it cannot be manufactured, it does not come by conscious, moral effort. "It is by God's grace that you have been saved, through faith. It is not your own doing, but God's gift. There is nothing here to boast of, since it is not the result of your own efforts" (Ephesians 2:8-9).

In Revelation 3:16, Jesus pictures himself as one knocking on the door of every human life. He promises those who become aware of him that if they open the door, and make room for him in their lives, he will enter and live within them in a most intimate personal relationship. God's role is to attract our attention and, when we respond, come to reside within us by his Spirit. Our role is to listen when he speaks to us and humbly, without reservation, invite him to take over the business of running our lives. From that point, we belong to him. We take him into account in every decision and desire his will for us above our own. God never pressures us to make this most critical of decisions. He could break down the door but he wants us to be his beloved friends, not his frightened slaves.

Receiving Jesus Christ into our lives is a matter of faith—faith in God's word and Jesus' character. It is not a matter of our being "good enough" to merit God's favor. It is not a matter of "feeling" that something has happened. When we ask Jesus to come into our lives we have done our part in the salvation process, and we must believe that he will do his part: he *will* come and reside within us the moment we ask him sincerely to do so. We may not see flashing lights or hear bells ring; we may not feel very much at all (although we might).

So, don't look at your feelings, look at his promise. If you have done your part, God will surely do his and you need only believe it. Thank him that he has now taken up residence in your life because he promised to do it. Be happy about it. You are a new creature, a child of God, born into his family, whether you feel it or not, whether you begin to show it right away or you don't.

A newborn baby doesn't understand very much, it doesn't see things very clearly, its emotions aren't very highly tuned. However, as the child grows and begins to try to do the things that he sees are expected of him, things his entire system strives after, he begins to comprehend more, to appreciate more, to raise questions, to try to discover the best and easiest ways to do things.

So it is with the newborn Christian! You will not be able to run the four-minute-mile! There will be much that confuses or disappoints you, much that you seem unable to accomplish. You will have old habits that refuse to die, old desires that will not give up and go away. However, within you is a new Life which hungers to please God, to walk in his footsteps. It is your daily task to nourish that new life in order that it may grow, blossom, and bear fruit until you begin to resemble God's Son, the Captain of your salvation, the Prince of the kings of the earth.

If you are eager to grow "to the very height of Christ's full stature" (Ephesians 4:13), this book is written for you. You can encourage the life of God in you, or stifle it; nourish it, or let it die. If you choose God's answers, and decide to do things God's way, his Spirit in you will flourish. God will do his thing in you if you will permit him to do so, if you will obey him, love him, and keep yourself open to his instruction and his love. God has a purpose for each life, and complete salvation comes when you allow him to have his way and make of you what he wishes. It's never easy because saying "yes" to God means saying "no" to yourself. The promise to those who persist is joy abundant and life everlasting.

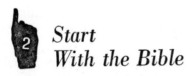

Start
With the Bible

STUDYING IS painful, but, sometimes, the results make the pain worthwhile.

Jesus said, "If you continue in my word, you are truly my disciples, and you will know the truth and the truth will make you free" (John 8:31, 32 RSV). The Bible is central and indispensable because it is the record of Jesus' words, of God's truth. Without it we can't be free.

You, undoubtedly, have had the experience of trying to make your way through a dark room without switching on the light. You thought you knew where everything was. But—ow!—that table shouldn't have been there! and—oh!— that chair must be out of place! and—crash!—there goes the lamp! and—screech!—you've stumbled onto the cat. Soon, you're aching in a dozen places and the whole family is awake.

One of the psalms says "Thy word is a lamp to my feet and a light to my path" (Psalm 119:105 RSV). Without the light of the Bible we keep banging into things. With it, we see things as they really are, not as we imagine them to be. The Bible gives us the truth. Apart from it, all we have is opinion.[1]

The Bible is not just a description of the way things are; it is also a book of promises about the way things can be. On almost every page you'll find one or two mind-bending promises about what God can do in your life IF. . . . Check it out! Promise, after promise, after promise—almost every one with a set of conditions. "*If* you do this, then that will surely follow." Notice the quotation at the bottom of page 3. In a day in which freedom is being demanded in every imaginable sphere of life, Jesus promises to give us freedom. But, there's a condition: "if you continue in my word." Christians who don't know that word will not be free. It is as simple as that.

Promise, after promise, will go unfulfilled in your life unless you know those promises and act on them. When God promises to do something if certain conditions are met and you fulfill those conditions, you can expect him to do his part. For example, he says "Come to me, all of you who are tired from carrying your heavy loads, and I will give you rest" (Matthew 11:28). We all want a restful spirit; we want to be free from the problems and troubles that we carry around with us. What does Jesus say we must do to get this rest? Come to him! Yet, what do we do usually when we feel burdened? We complain to friends, raid the ice box, indulge in favorite escape activities, or make matters worse through endless introspection. Jesus says that if we take our troubles to him (and leave them there!) our hearts will be filled with peace. Try it next time!

The Bible says that "in all things God works for good with those who love him. . ." (Romans 8:28). Do you love God? Have you given him your life to do with as he pleases? If you have, why are you fretting over the difficult circumstances you find yourself in? God assures those who love him that *everything* in their lives is engineered by him for their own good. God knows what he is doing. Trust his word and stop chafing and complaining.

The Bible is not a book of bite-sized blessings. It is an immensely practical handbook of specific instruction in the truth that liberates. Are you fearful and anxious? Read I John. Do you have financial and material needs? Check out Matthew 6 and believe it! Are you being tempted? Read I Corinthians 10. Jesus said "*continue* in my word, and so you shall be my disciples."

The word "disciple" means "learner" (note its similarity to the word "discipline"). Jesus wants us to be disciplined students of his word and that brings up the question of motivation. It is one thing to get your spiritual kicks on Jesus; it is quite another to be his serious follower.

Sooner or later you have to come to grips with the fact that you are under attack at this very point.[2] You have a spiritual enemy called the devil, or Satan, whose purposes are directly contrary to those of God. If God considers the Bible crucial to us, the devil is going to do all he can to keep us from it. Think for a moment of the kinds of excuses you allow to come between you and your daily Bible study: there isn't enough time; you don't "feel" like it; you can't seem to find a quiet place without interruptions; it's so hard to concentrate; you don't want to do it out of a sense of obligation; and on, and on.

Nonsense—and trivial nonsense at that! Yet, there is probably no problem in the Christian life that more people struggle with than that of regular, daily, Bible study and prayer. We're ready to do great things for God but we can't find fifteen minutes a day to study the Bible. Why? Because it's the light, and the devil doesn't want us to walk in the light. The devil will do everything in his power to keep us in darkness. The Bible is the truth; without it we cannot be free. The devil will do all he can to keep us in bondage.

Don't think I'm making too much of this. The devil tempted Jesus *when he was trying to be alone with God.* Note carefully that the temptation came in the form of twisted scripture. If Jesus hadn't known the Bible well enough to answer the devil with scripture, and if he hadn't been absolutely committed to obeying it, he would have wiped out before he got started. So will you.

Paul wrote to Timothy, "study to show yourself approved unto God, a workman who doesn't need to be ashamed, who rightly handles the word of truth" (II Timothy 2:15 RSV). Decide to study, commit yourself to doing it, and stick to it, in spite of all temptations and rationalizations. Say "no!" to your laziness; stop coddling your feelings. Mean business and the battle is largely won. Discipleship is this: determining to do whatever is necessary, even if it hurts, to prove your allegiance to Jesus.

Here are a few practical suggestions: 1) Find, or make, a good quiet place where you won't be disturbed. 2) Allow enough time really to get something done. These two may mean getting up before the rest of the family (or dormitory), which may mean going to bed early enough the night before to respond to the alarm clock. 3) Ask God to help you concentrate, to help you to push distractions out of your mind. Ask him to open your understanding by his Spirit so that you will find your study exciting. 4) Decide what you'll study ahead of time and stick to it. Don't open the Bible haphazardly and hope to get "blessed" each day. Someone once said "he who aims at nothing is sure to hit it!" 5) Use a good, modern translation such as *Good News for Modern Man*. This is the New Testament in very readable form and can be obtained from most book stores for about fifty cents. 6) Look for specifics. Is there a command to be obeyed in the passage you are reading? a sin to be renounced? an example to be followed? a promise you can claim? a condition to be met if the promise is to be fulfilled? Apply these to your own life. 7) Keep a notebook of the things you learn and ask God to help you remember and act on them.

There is so much false teaching going around (often in the name of Christ) that God himself is going to have to be our teacher. He wants to be that, if we will be his students. Ask the Holy Spirit to prepare you, enlighten your mind, make you receptive and attentive, and help you apply what you learn. With the Spirit's help the Bible can become the most exciting, helpful, encouraging book you will ever read. Studying may be painful but sometimes its results make the pain worthwhile.

NOTES

[1] Note that we will be discussing all of the supporting reasons for our confidence in the Bible's reliability in Chapter 13.

[2] We will have a good deal more to say about this in Chapters 7 and 17.

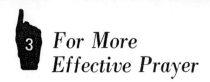

3 For More Effective Prayer

BEFORE YOU became a Christian, you had some experience in praying—mainly the panic-button sort or the gimme-gimme variety. As a Christian you know the Lord personally, and it is only natural that you would expect prayer to be something very special, a two-way communication with God, the means by which you draw divine power into everyday life.

Because prayer is a dynamic experience, it cannot be programmed. However, the prayer sessions which will prove most meaningful to you will probably include *praise, confession, thanksgiving, intercession, and petition.* Let's imagine that you are about to begin a time of prayer; you have found a quiet, private place where interruptions are unlikely and you are determined to resist the sleepiness or mental distractions which will undoubtedly creep in to hinder you. You have found a position which is just comfortable enough so as not to become a liability!

Begin with *praise.* Focus your mind on God, your Father in Heaven, and let yourself be touched with an awareness of his incredible power. He is the One responsible for the galaxies of space, the power of crashing waves, the perfection of the butterfly, and the wonder of daisies and willows, and he loves you. He reached out in love towards you long before you ever desired him; his thoughts towards you are thoughts of pleasure and delight, not of condemnation. Tell this wonderful God that you love him. Praise him in your spirit; fight the impulse to pass over this portion of prayer and hurry on to more pressing things. The mighty prayers recorded in the Bible are invariably filled with grateful adoration of God and appreciation of all that he is and has done. If, at first, you have difficulty considering God, think about Jesus, remember the radiant love and buoyant power that surged through him as he healed and preached in ancient Palestine. Ponder his love for you, his lack of fear, his authority and courage in the face of hostility and threats. Rejoice that he considered you important enough to die for, so important that he suffered extreme humiliation and degradation, as well as pain, in order that you might be washed of your sins and given new life. Let the memory of Jesus humble you and produce a longing to cast yourself before him in worship and adoration.

Next, with a humble and contrite heart, *confess* your sins to God. Ask the Holy Spirit within you to help you remember and admit any sins, mistakes, or wrong attitudes that need to be dealt with. Ask the Spirit to help you understand why you sinned, and how you can avoid it in the future. Be especially sensitive to any resentments or jealousy you may have towards other people. Jesus specifically commanded us to clear all accounts with other people before we approach God. Be ruthlessly honest about yourself, but remember always that God is not ruthless with you, but very gentle and full of patience and forgiveness.

It is important that you do not let this concentration on your sins discourage you, make you angry or frustrated. You are to "walk in the light" but you must not let shock at what you see overwhelm you. The purpose of confession is that you may be thoroughly and completely forgiven, knowing the joy of being clean and guiltless before God. His word promises that "if we confess our sins, he is faithful and just to forgive us our sins and cleanse us from all unrighteousness" (I John 1:9 KJV). If you've confessed, then he has forgiven and cleansed! Believe it! Corrie Ten Boom says "Cast your sins into the sea of God's forgetfulness, and then put up a sign that says 'no fishing allowed!' "

Thanksgiving should follow confession. Thank God that you are forgiven, and soon you will feel forgiven, for feelings follow faith in spiritual matters. Rejoice that you are accepted utterly by the Father, just as you are with all your mistakes, faults, sins, and tendency to get into trouble. Thank him for everything that brings you joy. Thank him for the future he has planned for you. Thank him for the unexpected ways he is going to meet you today, and for the fact that he is going to answer your prayers and meet your needs. Thank him as well for the things you don't understand, for the circumstances that look confusing or cause you fear. We are told "always give thanks *for everything* to God the Father in the name of our Lord Jesus Christ" (Ephesians 5:20). As you thank him for the bad things, you will begin to sense that they, too, are in his hands and he can bring wonderful things out of them if you will trust him with them.

Every prayer-time should include *intercession* for the needs of others. Praying for others is training in love. Ask the Spirit to bring to your mind those people you should pray for (you might like to use a prayer list, if you prefer, as an aid) and ask to see them as God sees them. Consider each one individually with an uncritical heart and pray as you begin to see his needs. As you ask God to release, help, heal, or save him, be willing to be his instrument in his life. Are you willing truly to befriend that person, sacrificing your time for him? Are you willing to initiate talk with him about the things of God? Could you just listen and accept him if that is what God seems to want? If God has given you a prayer-concern for someone, it is an indication that God is using you already in that person's life. Pray for love and discernment.

Remember: when you have brought someone to God in prayer, leave him there! God loves your friend or family member more than you do. You should not come away from intercession heavyhearted for that indicates that you have no faith that God has heard and cares. Have you given him to God? Then he has him! Rejoice—and stop fretting!

Petition for your own needs is where it's at for most of you. Your problems loom large and often make it hard to pray for anyone else. However, God has assured you that it is appropriate for you to pray about yourselves and all your needs, large and small.

Jesus gave his disciples some wonderful prayer-principles which we should begin to apply to our own prayers. He said:

The Father will give you anything you ask of him . . . (John 16:23)

If you remain in me, and my words remain in you, then you will ask for anything you wish, and you shall have it. (John 15:7)

And whatever you ask in prayer you will receive, if you have faith. (Matthew 21:22, RSV)

There are three important prayer-secrets here: the prayer "in Jesus' name"; the prayer of the truly committed disciple; the prayer of faith.

First, you are told that you can ask for anything if you do so "in Jesus' name." That doesn't mean that you tack that phrase on to the end of every request, thus insuring its fulfillment. It means that you are daring to approach the Father trusting in the character and merit of Jesus, not in your own worth or righteousness. It is rather like the ambassador from Great Britain, who approaches the President of France "in the name of" the Queen. The ambassador is not the Queen, and in himself has little distinction. However, the throne he represents has power and significance and he is relying entirely upon that. When we pray "in Jesus' name" we are claiming to be in the service of Jesus whom God, himself, raised "to the highest place above, and gave him the name that is greater than any other name. So that all beings in heaven, on earth, and in the world below will fall on their knees in honor of the name of Jesus"

(Philippians 2:9-10). When we pray in the name of Jesus, even the demons of hell take notice. Jesus' name has sufficient power to compel lame legs to mend and dead bodies to rise. When Peter commanded the lame man to walk in Acts 3, he explained it later in this manner to the crowd that gathered: "It was the power of his name that gave strength to this lame man. What you see and know was done by faith in his name" (Acts 3:16). Begin to stand in reverent awe of the name of Jesus and to believe that by its power and through faith in its bearer great things can be accomplished.

Jesus said, also, that you can ask for anything you want "if you remain in me, and my words remain in you." Why? Because if you are grafted into Jesus like a branch into a parent vine, his very nature is in you and your desires and interests are in accord with his. Are you abiding in him with tenacious, determined trust? Do you study and "keep" his Word, seeking constantly to obey it and remember it? If you do all this, you are not likely to seek from God that which is sinful and dangerous and you can trust your desires and make your requests.

Finally, you are told to pray in faith. "If you believe, you will receive whatever you ask for in prayer" (Matthew 21:22). Faith is something every Christian possesses. But you need to learn to use that faith more effectively. Faith is like a spiritual muscle—the more you use it the stronger it gets. As you learn more about your authority and power as a child of God, your faith will grow and you will dare to trust God for bigger things. Great feats of faith can be tackled only after smaller ones have been mastered. Your faith may be strained if you attempt too much, too soon. Don't talk yourself into believing things that you really, deep down, don't believe. This "positive thinking" approach will fail because it is not really faith at all.

I remember praying for months that a friend would not

die of cancer. I shut my mind to the nagging realization that she was losing ground. I said "thank you, Lord, that she will live!" even when I didn't believe it. When my friend died, it seemed to me that I had cared more about her than God had and I had trouble overcoming bitterness and despair. I had tried too much, too soon; I didn't have the "muscle" to claim that much in faith.

That doesn't mean I should not have prayed. However, there's a difference between "asking" prayer and "believing" prayer. Jesus, himself, asked God, in his neediest hour, that his death might be prevented. He did not "claim" continued life. He placed his request in a larger context: "not what I want, but what you want" (Matthew 26:39). He had learned to distinguish between those things that he wanted (but was willing to submit to God's greater purposes), and those things he knew that God intended to do (which he then claimed in faith). When you lack the assurance from God's Spirit that something is definitely his will and therefore yours to claim, you should not try to claim it. You may, however, certainly ask for it and, perhaps, even as you do, God will give you inner conviction that you will receive it. In the end, your trust is in God, not in your own faith, and you can leave the results to him. As your faith grows, you will be able to see God's purposes and power more clearly and pray believing-prayer more frequently. And then "you will be able to say to this hill, 'Get up and throw yourself into the sea' and it will!" (Matthew 21:21).

An example of believing-prayer came to me a few years ago, when I was responsible for a winter conference that never came off due to lack of snow and I was left owing $250 to the lodge and the printers. Being a student, I had no money on hand and none in sight. As I prayed about it, I felt God give me great confidence and peace, he seemed to be saying "Don't worry, I'll take care of it." "Lord," I said, "I feel certain that you want me to claim this promise. Thank you for providing for this need." Saying "thank you" ahead of time bolstered my faith.

The next day I spoke to a group of church women. After my speech, one of them came up to me. "As I was praying for you this morning, I felt that the Lord wanted me to give you this," she said, handing me an envelope. Inside was a check for $250.

Sometimes your needs are so great that you may feel unable to pray about them with power and confidence. It is time then for group prayer. "Whenever two of you on earth agree about anything you pray for, it will be done for you by my Father in heaven" (Matthew 18:19). I prayed with a group of Christian ministers for the infant son of one of them who was dying of a rare, "incurable" disease. Although my own faith-muscles were weak, the boldness of others was a great encouragement and day by day we became more confident that God was going to do a mighty thing in spite of the doctor's growing pessimism. Finally, when it appeared that he could hold out no longer, there was a reversal so abrupt and inexplicable that the doctors called it a miracle. Alone, none of us could have believed God sufficiently for that, but together we were empowered to claim it.

Joint prayer is extremely helpful if you are struggling with an area of obedience. If God has told you clearly to give up something, or if there is something you are supposed to do but cannot, it is humbling but helpful to find another Christian and admit your difficulty to him. Then, together, ask God to help you overcome your resistance to his will and find the strength to obey. "Confess your sins to one another, and pray for one another, so that you will be healed" (James 5:16). You need other people. If you hide behind "Christian" masks or play religious games or pray in order to impress others you are making a mockery of prayer. But with humility, honesty, and confidence in God's promises, joint prayer can be the greatest source of spiritual power you will ever discover.

A distinction should be made here between praying about problems and praying for desires. A different approach is appropriate to each.

When you take a problem to God, trust that he has it. Don't continue to fret. Either you have given it to him or you haven't. Either he is capable of handling it or he isn't. If you have, and since he is, let it go and relax. Trust that it is being taken care of and refuse to yield to a desire to keep worrying. If you took your watch to a master repairman, you wouldn't stand outside his door pacing the floor, snatching it back every hour to check on it.

When you have a deep desire for something, don't be afraid to ask—persistently! God is delighted to find Christians who are determined to get an answer. Once, while describing prayer, Jesus spoke of a widow who beat incessantly on a judge's door until, exasperated, he gave in and granted her request. Jesus also told about a man who refused to take "no" for an answer when he needed a favor from one of his neighbors. God isn't reluctant to hear us, nor exasperated at our petitioning, but these stories tell you that your earnestness and determination is a factor in his taking your prayers seriously. Afer all, what pleasure is there in feeding someone who refuses to get hungry? "Open thy mouth *wide* and I will fill it!" (Psalm 81:10 KJV). God wants to satisfy you, but he wants you to be serious and persistent. "Seek and ye shall find, ask and ye shall receive, knock and the door will be opened. For those who seek, find; those who ask, receive; and the door will be opened to those who knock" (Matthew 7:7-8 KJV). What do you want from God—spiritual gifts? power to be a bold, effective witness? more love for others? a marriage partner? financial help? healing? If you are asking anything amiss, God will show you. However, if the request seems legitimate, keep at it! And, of course, be patient. Many times God must make deep changes in you (and others) by his Spirit before he can grant you the desires of your heart.

Then, we should all remember what the word "Amen" means. It means "so be it!" or 'that's the way it's going to be!" When you end your prayers with "amen," you are voicing your confidence that your prayers have been heard and you are expecting God to act. "Amen" is not an "I-hope-so" word; it is an "I-know-so" word. Your faith will grow if you remember its meaning when you use it.

Let prayer be an adventure for you. It is a means of getting to know God by seeing him act in response to your requests; a means of accomplishing mighty things in your life and the lives of others. "Lord, teach us to pray!" Amen!

4 Guidance: How To Hear God Speaking

NOT LONG ago a friend wrote:

I understand about getting general moral guidance from the Bible, but what about specifics? Charlie said that the Lord had guided him personally about Sally and dating. How does God guide like that? Could he guide me about college? How can I tell when it is God and not just myself?

God *can* guide about college, and about how to spend your summer vacation, and whether to join that fraternity or to room with this person or that one.

If you have tried to get guidance on such matters but seem to have difficulty hearing God's voice, there are three questions you should ask yourself:

First: are you listening? Our toddler manages to "hear" us only when she wants to. She is skilled in tuning us out when we're giving orders she doesn't want to obey. She doesn't do this consciously; she is not deliberately defying us. She just automatically shifts into deaf gear when she detects a certain tone in the voice that tells her we are about to intrude. Have you been ignoring God like that? You can't presume to tune God in only when you want answers to your questions. If you want him to speak to you, you must be willing to listen to him—on all matters. Has God been speaking to you about obedience in some area of your life while you have been blithely oblivious? Ask his Spirit to help you hear him.

Second: do you obey? When you *do* know that God is trying to say something to you, even if you think it's silly, do you respond promptly? The more you obey, the better you hear. The most effective remedy for faulty hearing in spiritual matters is obedience to what you have already heard.

Third: are you willing? Are you *really* willing to have God interfere with your pet interests? Are you really willing to allow him to have his way even when it goes against your natural inclinations or might cause a critical reaction from someone close to you? Until you let go of your own will, you will not receive guidance from God. He does not tell you his will and permit you the luxury of rejecting it. When you accept his will before knowing it, then he will speak to you.

How, exactly, does God speak? He communicates with us through his Holy Spirit within us; through older, more experienced Christians; through the Bible; through our circumstances; through a combination of all of these. Sometimes he does not speak at all and we must simply trust him, and use our own judgment. Let's look at each of these:

God's Spirit

Every Christian is indwelt by the Holy Spirit, who is a Person with will, feelings, and the ability to communicate.

The Bible says he can be grieved, resisted, quenched, vexed, or obeyed. His function is to teach, lead, empower, comfort, and strengthen us. The Holy Spirit can speak audibly within us but this occurs rarely. Usually, he speaks softly through inner impressions or nudges and his guidance is always directed towards blessing or helping you or other people. The Holy Spirit does not shout nor force us to pay attention to him. It is not too difficult to ignore him altogether, or to persuade yourself that your "leadings" are not really from God. Again, the key is willingness. (First ask the Holy Spirit to remove the idea entirely if it is not part of his will for you.) Then, when you are willing to do God's thing, your fear will dwindle and you will have the inner assurance that it is, indeed, God who is speaking to you.

Some of the Holy Spirit's gifts are helpful in providing guidance. These are usually manifested most powerfully in group prayer meetings where the gifts of tongues and interpretation, or the gift of prophecy, could be the means by which the Spirit gives you clear, specific guidance. This is discussed more fully in the chapter on the Holy Spirit and his gifts (chapter 18).

Holy Spirit guidance is essential as an inward confirmation of guidance received through other means. God may use the following means of communication with you. However, he will always assure you that the guidance is from him by giving you inner peace from his Spirit as you consider the leadings you have received.

Christian Advice

Usually, a young Christian has one or more older, more experienced Christians given to him as shepherds and teachers in the faith. Those who have walked with God are more familiar with his ways than you are and God often uses their gifts and wisdom to guide you, a young Christian.

Sometimes it is hard to humble yourself and admit you need help. Perhaps, that is the reason God so frequently uses the help of older Christians to guide younger ones in their decisions. However, as you receive their advice, expect the Spirit to give you inner assurance that it is, indeed, from God. If this is lacking, wait.

Guidance through circumstances

God can engineer our circumstances. He will place us in situations in order to teach us, or to use us. Sometimes he permits us to run off into sinful or difficult experiences in order to bring us to deeper humility and obedience. God can open doors and shut gates, hedge us in or push us out, by dealing with the people and conditions around us.

There are some fascinating stories in the Bible about God's intervention in human circumstances. Christians often speak of "laying a fleece" before the Lord. This term comes from the story of Gideon who was frightened of the task he thought God was giving him and wanted to be absolutely sure it was God's idea before he began it. So he asked God to keep the evening dew from wetting a piece of lambs-wool he placed outdoors overnight. The next morning it was dry as a bone in the middle of drenched ground. Being skeptical, and very reluctant, Gideon tried it again the next night, reversing the instructions. When he found the fleece wet and the ground dry, he gave in and did what God asked. God is patient with tests like this and many times they are the only means we have of knowing God's will with assurance.

Often your circumstances reveal God's will by the effect they have on your walk with God. If a friendship, job, attitude, or habit hinders your spiritual growth, that is ample reason for stopping it. A detrimental effect is a form of guidance.

A teenage girl wrote recently saying, "I am praying that God will give me some sign as to whether or not I should break up with Roger." Her relationship with Roger causes her to sin, to miss out on meetings and services where she could be gaining important knowledge about God, and she thinks of him an inordinate amount of time. God has *already* given her ample signs about this relationship! Is there anything in your life that is preoccupying you or hindering you to the extent that you are not going on with God as you should?

The Bible

Scripture speaks with authority on many subjects. Use a topical Bible guide and look up your area of concern to learn what the Bible says about it. For instance, if you are considering marriage, have you read all of the Biblical passages about it and about the role of man and woman in Christian marriage?

God cannot contradict himself, so if you think you have received guidance that goes against scriptural revelation—you haven't. A person who says God led him to marry a non-Christian, or to lie, or to indulge in drunkenness or sexual promiscuity, is mistaken because God has clearly spoken against these things in scripture. Get to know your Bible so that you can use it as a test, a standard by which to measure the guidance you may receive from other sources.

In closing this discussion, there is one warning which must be given. In Deuteronomy 18, the Lord lays great stress upon the importance of *not* seeking guidance apart from Christian sources. Astrology, fortune telling, ouija boards, palm or tea leaf reading, tarot cards, automatic writing, divination of any sort, seances or conjuring—all these are absolutely forbidden to the child of God. Those who practice such things are called "an abomination to the

Lord." There are forces in this world opposed to God who use these means eagerly to confuse or mislead a Christian. We are promised that "if any of you lacks wisdom, he should pray to God, who will give it to him; for God gives generously and graciously to all" (James 1:5). With a promise like that, why search elsewhere?

Life for the Christian is not so haphazard that you need ever fear even if your paths seem to be taking difficult or confusing turns. God is surely behind it and at the end of it as well! There are some times when he seems not to be speaking with clarity at all. Then, you are simply to trust his love and care, to believe that he will not let you go astray. Your ways are in his hand, and "the steps of a righteous man are ordered by the Lord" (Psalm 37:23 KJV). Trust that God is with you, exerting his influence upon your heart, will, mind and common sense, guiding with an unseen, unfelt hand. His promise "I will never leave you nor forsake you" (Deuteronomy 31:6 and Hebrews 13:5 KJV) is not conditional! He said it. He meant it. You believe it.

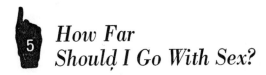

How Far Should I Go With Sex?

IN SPITE of the new problems we keep inventing to compete with it, sex continues to be the biggest hang-up during adolescence. Most young people want to know physical, sexual pleasure. They (especially the boys) want to experience for themselves the much-publicized excitement that sexual fulfillment provides. They want it when they want it, which is most of the time. They want it without a lot of hassle or guilt; they don't want to have to think about it, or worry about it very deeply. Young people (especially the girls) also want to be the ones who bestow this pleasure on others, those they want to delight and captivate. They see no reason for denying themselves this ultimate in physical pleasure, nor do they wish to be accused of denying it to others who regard it as a supreme proof of affection. Everything in their culture convinces young people that sexual gratification is the pearl of great price which Puritan ethics and social taboos have denied them for too long. They are told that they need not feel guilty about sexual indulgence. Yet, it is our experience that sexual guilt has *not* been eradicated in countless young lives.

What is the Christian view of sex? The Bible teaches that, in God's eyes, it is far more than a sensual pleasure or a means of begetting children; it is the outward sign of two people who have joined themselves together for life (Genesis 2:24). Indeed it is much more than that. St. Paul goes so far as to say that sexual intercourse is a type, or picture, of a far more important union, the union of God's Spirit with those who belong to him by faith (Ephesians 5:21-33). Your union with God involves the commitment of your entire self for your entire lifetime—and throughout eternity. It is to be a public commitment, something you acknowledge before men (Matthew 10:32-33). In the same way, your sexual union is only to be an expression of deep, loving, lifetime commitment, publicly announced through the rite of marriage. When two people are joined in marriage, they openly vow their love and determination to live the rest of their lives as one unit. This oneness is symbolized and sealed by the act of sexual intercourse, just as their commitment to God is sealed and assured when he sends his Spirit to live in their hearts and they become one with him through faith (Romans 7:4). When men defile marriage by encouraging sexual union apart from the responsibilities and commitments which make marriage what it is, they are scorning the deeper, more profound union with God which marriage is intended to symbolize.

It is difficult for modern man to see marriage as *the* important thing, because culture has conditioned him to think that sex is what marriage is all about. The Bible, however, regards sex as only one aspect of the marriage relationship, and not the most important one at that. If, in fact, husband and wife are not providing each other with the respect, concern, love, and security which, at times, human beings need more profoundly than they need sexual satisfaction, there is every reason to suspect that their sexual life will be disappointing as well. Marriage is God's way of providing the necessary ingredients which can enable two people to find the ultimate in sexual pleasure. Psychiatrist's offices are filled with people who are deeply troubled because they have tried to find in sexual relationships outside of marriage the fulfillment of their deepest needs, needs which cannot be met by sex alone. Sex without security, without the leisure and relaxed atmosphere that only marriage can provide, is far less pleasurable than God intended it to be. The Bible commands the Christian to believe this —and wait.

It is not very strange to suppose that sex apart from marriage is inadequate. Even most teenagers want more than sex. They want love, *real* love, love so strong and permanent that it can be affirmed with vows of eternal fidelity. Modern songs reveal a hunger for commitment as the framework within which sex finds its proper place. You do not really want something cheap and superficial and transient; you crave that which is secure and lasting. You want the kind of relationship where you can know and be known, in which you accept and are accepted just as you are. You want to give yourself fully to a person who gives himself or herself fully to you, and not just in physical terms. In short, you want *commitment*. And that means marriage.

If your love is not deep enough to become marriage-love, then it is not deep enough for sex. That's why the so-called "trial marriage" is a contradiction in terms. If it is a marriage, it's a lifetime commitment; if it's a trial, it isn't. Sex must be enjoyed within the framework of a commitment that is "for better, for worse, for richer, for poorer, in sickness and in health, to love and to cherish till death us do part. . . ."

A student once told us, "My idea of the perfect evening was to make it with two girls because everybody else was only making it with one. Then, I met a girl I respected as much as I desired, and suddenly I wished sex could be something special, something sacred."

That's the tragedy: you can't have it both ways. It is impossible to make "special" something that has become "common." The Bible says that sex is very special, so special that it belongs only to that one special love, that one person to whom you give so much more than your body, to whom you pledge your life. Save it for that.

"But," someone may say, "suppose two people are engaged, they know they are going to get married anyway—what's wrong with sex beforehand?" Sex is part of a larger commitment. If for some reason that commitment can't yet be assumed publicly and all its responsibilities accepted, there is no justification for grabbing this particular benefit of married life ahead of time. If their current circumstances prevent two people from getting married, how can they be certain that these circumstances will not prevent them from *ever* getting married? If they are going to get married anyway, why don't they? We have seen several instances where Christian couples knew that it was God's will for them to marry and, rather than endure the unbearable anguish of further delay, they trusted God to help them make an earlier marriage possible. The Holy Spirit is a splendid marriage counselor. Nothing is impossible once it is placed in God's hands.

A persistent argument in favor of premarital sex is that it is necessary if a person is to become expert enough in sexual matters to be a successful husband or wife. Not long ago a student challenged his minister who had just given a talk on sex: "Some of us have already slept with more than half a dozen girls, while you've limited yourself to just one. Maybe *we* should be instructing *you*." The minister smiled, took out a pencil, and did some figuring on an envelope. In a moment he said "I've been married for ten years. Most married couples have sex together between three and four times a week. Assuming we're typical that means my wife and I have had sex something over eighteen hundred times and we're still learning about its subtlety, richness and joy. Now, how much experience did you say you've had?"

Question: What makes you a better musician, dabbling with one instrument after another, or sticking with one instrument until you know the full range of its capability and you've become almost one with it? God wants you to enjoy your physical pleasures fully, and he knew that this could only be achieved when two people had a lifetime to discover the depth of pleasure inherent in sexual union. God is not trying to deprive you of pleasure by urging you to restrict sex to marriage; he is trying to help you find it most fully.

There's a very common argument being circulated these days which says that the Biblical teaching about sex is no longer valid because times have changed. According to this view, the Biblical position (no sex outside of marriage) was based on *fear*—fear of unwanted pregnancy, venereal disease, or the social stigma attached to getting caught at it—summed up as "conception, infection, detection." And, the argument has it, because we've solved these problems—

we've got the Pill, penicillin, and most people couldn't care less anyway—the ethic that was based on the fear of these problems may be forgotten.

We might note in passing that we've hardly "solved" these problems. In spite of the Pill, there were over 100,000 abortions in New York City alone in 1970; in spite of penicillin, venereal disease is at a record high for the history of the world; the Playboy philosophy notwithstanding, a great many people do care very much.

Interestingly enough, however, you can search the Scriptures from cover to cover and you'll not find a single instance in which the strictures against sex outside of marriage are couched in any of these terms. The Biblical injunctions are not to prevent what might go wrong, but to protect what should go right; not because sex outside of marriage is so bad, but because sex inside of marriage can be so good—and because you can't have it both ways. Once you've taken what was special and used it as if it weren't, there's no way you can make it special again.

Perhaps the most common objection raised today by young people against the Biblical position is that sex and love go together and since love is so marvelous sex must be permitted in order to maintain and, hopefully, increase love. We recently received a phone call from a sobbing teenage girl who had just slept with a boy for the first time. No, she didn't love him—not yet. Why did she do it? "Well, he loves me, and he wanted it so much, and it would have been really unloving of me if I'd turned him down. I just didn't want to hurt him."

There's a strange and poignant story in the Old Testament about two twin brothers, the eldest of whom, Esau, was due to inherit from his father the birthright blessing which would entitle him to the Promised Land and perpetual greatness. In a moment of weakness, however, he thoughtlessly sold his birthright to his younger brother,

Jacob, for a bowl of stew. For a momentary pleasure, Esau sold the most precious possesion he had. And God said, "Jacob I have loved, but Esau I have hated" (Romans 9:13 KJV). God has given human beings a great privilege, and we honor deeply the one to whom we first give ourselves. To cheapen and degrade ourselves by giving our bodies to satisfy the temporary passions of boyfriends or girlfriends or to avoid peer pressure and social ostracism is a tragedy that occurs much too frequently in modern America. "Love" at age fifteen is not what it will be at age twenty-one. Love is not the god to whom we sacrifice our moral standards. We have a God in heaven who has told us clearly what to do.

The Biblical view is under such incessant attack that it seemed necessary to discuss it and its detractors in detail. However, for most of us, the real issue is not theoretical, but practical: How far *should* I go, and how do I deal with temptations to go farther?

Unfortunately, the Bible does not give you the kind of formula you might wish for. It sets absolute limits: You shall not commit adultery (Exodus 20:14); flee fornication (I Corinthians 6:18 KJV); have nothing to do with homosexuality (Romans 1:26, 27). It tells you that God is even concerned with your thought life (Matthew 5:27). Then, it lets it go.

The question, "How far should I go?" is really a question of our motivation for going anywhere at all. Marriage manuals and medical textbooks call even the most minimal physical intimacy "foreplay"—that is, the preliminary activity designed to lead to complete sexual union. Indulging in any petting or "making out," without "going all the way" is, thus, one of the most frustrating things you can do. By its very nature it is designed to prepare for something more and, if you don't intend to see it through, why start at all? That's not to suggest, however, that engaged people need necessarily restrict themselves to what is appropriate on the first date. It is to recognize that the intensity of physical contact grows irresistibly and irreversibly and the farther you go the farther you will want to go. Why risk creating pressures for yourselves that you cannot handle, or, worse, creating them for the one you are dating? We have witnessed the anguish and guilt of Christian couples who have gone too far and want to return to a relationship which is not dominated by sex. They discover that backtracking is extremely difficult and with each renewed effort at self-control their guilt is increased terribly if they fail, and failure is not uncommon. The value of a chaste relationship is becoming increasingly more evident to us each year.

How, then, can these problems be avoided? First, think the matter through ahead of time. Most mistakes are made in the heat of the moment when a lack of predetermined principles allows "feelings" to dictate. Avoid situations you know will be tempting. Perhaps there is real wisdom in dating only other Christians who will agree with your moral reservations. God has no law about this, but he does make it clear that Christians are to *marry* only other Christians (II Corinthians 6:14). If you don't want to "fall in love" with someone who is not a Christian, why pursue a relationship that could lead to love? This is a hard matter which you will have to pray and ask God about. It could mean no dating at all for a time.

In dating, in selecting college living units and roommates, in agreeing to social appointments, and in your private thought life shun that which stimulates desires appropriate only to marriage. In books, films, and conversations, avoid whatever cheapens and degrades that which God has given. If you find yourself being tempted, *get up and leave*. Forcibly turn your mind towards something else.

"He who walks righteously . . . and shuts his eyes from looking upon evil, he will dwell on the heights (Isaiah

33:15 RSV). "Fill your minds with those things that are good and deserve praise; things that are true, noble, right, pure, lovely, and honorable" (Philippians 4:8). "My deep desire is that I shall never fail in my duty . . . so that with my whole self I shall bring honor to Christ" (Philippians 1:20). "Come out from among them and be ye separate, saith the Lord" (II Corinthians 6:17 KJV). Glorify God in your body (I Corinthians 6:20).

Mistakes in the area of sex are not unforgivable, and they are not the worst possible mistakes you can make. If you have already failed in this area, confess, repent, and believe God for your forgiveness. With God's help, determine never to fail again. Jesus said that certain whores were closer to God's kingdom than certain of the Pharisees. Of course, it's better to be neither.

6 Drugs and Drink

LET'S FIRST be clear about what the Bible does *not* say. Nowhere does it condemn alcohol—in fact, at one point it recommends taking a little wine "to help your digestion" (I Timothy 5:23). It doesn't even mention drugs. There is, however, a good deal in the Scriptures which ought to influence our behavior in both of these areas. The case against drugs and liquor is especially strong for the teen-ager on two counts.

First, *drunkenness*. While the Bible does not prohibit alcoholic drinking, it condemns resoundingly getting drunk in both the Old and the New Testaments. Isaiah, one of Israel's greatest prophets, said: "those who reel with wine and stagger with strong drink . . . err in vision, they stumble in giving judgement. [Therefore] they shall be trodden underfoot" (Isaiah 28:3, 7 RSV). The apostle Paul put it even more strongly when he wrote, "human nature ... shows itself in immoral, filthy, and indecent actions .... People ... get drunk, have orgies, and do other things like these. I warn you now as I have before: those who do these things will not receive the Kingdom of God" (Galatians 5:19-21). In writing to the Romans, he said, "Let us conduct ourselves properly, as people who live in the light of day; no orgies or drunkenness ... stop giving attention to your sinful nature, to satisfy its desires" (Romans 13:13, 14).

Drunkenness, according to the Biblical writers, is a great offence to God. The loss of self-control, the immodesty, the abuse to mind and body, and the general irresponsibility that accompanies drunkenness is considered disgraceful for the follower of Christ. The New Testament even goes so far as to command that we refuse to associate with fellow Christians who continually get drunk, because they defame Christ and should be rebuked (I Corinthians 5:11).

Today in America, the phenomenon of "social drinking" is an integral part of the way of life of most adults, something very much taken for granted. Many adults seem able to handle a cocktail before dinner, or brandy afterward, without any apparent ill-effects. At the same time, however, the problem of continual excess—of drunkenness and alcoholism—has reached such frightening proportions that a great number of Christians (and many others as well) have concluded that total abstinence is the only appropriate response.

Others, of course, feel that responsible moderation is equally appropriate. The Bible is very clear in saying that each man must decide such an issue for himself—under the guidance of the Holy Spirit—and that he must not pass judgment upon others (See Romans 14). *These are the only options: responsible moderation or total abstinence.*

For the teenager, there is special relevance in this. Perhaps an occasional glass of wine, at home, with your parents, or under similar circumstances, is permissible. The wild blast, the hidden drinking-for-the-sake-of-drinking, the unchaperoned party involving a raid on somebody's parents' bar, the turning of lights down low and records up high, the mixing of drinks with sex, the matching each other to see how many you can hold—none of these have any place in the life of a Christian.

As we turn from alcohol to other drugs, the issue is drawn ever more sharply. Even something as "mild" as marijuana smoking is virtually *aimed* at "blowing your mind," at "getting stoned"—in a word, at *drunkenness.*

This isn't to deny the differences between the "high" of marijuana and that of alcohol. With pot, there's a heightening, rather than a depressing, of the senses. With pot, there's no hang over. While it *may be* that our fears about the long-range medical effects of blowing grass are groundless (though physicians remain very much divided in their opinions about this), pot smoking may turn out to be a kind of Russian roulette that endangers not only yourself, but your children as well.

Even if *all* the fears could be answered adequately, however, the fact remains that the experience of pot smoking itself, to say nothing of taking "uppers" and "downers" and the even more seriously addicting drugs, consists of such a distortion of time and space, such a loss of control over emotions and actions, such a release of inhibitions, as to qualify precisely for the label of "drunkenness" that God so explicitly condemns.

The Christian is to keep his baser impulses under control and to be led by the Spirit of God. He is not simply to follow the crowd and be led by a spirit of revelry. Note Paul's contrast: "Do not get drunk with wine, which will only ruin you; instead be filled with the Spirit" (Ephesians

5:18). If he were writing today he would certainly say: "Keep off booze, pot, pills, a sniff of this, and a shot of that—why do you think they call it 'dope'? If you're looking for a 'high,' Jesus will lift your spirit as he fills you with his Spirit and he'll satisfy you as no trip on drugs can possibly do." The "peace of God" he wrote to the Philippians, will "keep your minds safe" (Philippians 4:9)— euphoriants will only distort them.

The second major issue goes far beyond the religious implications of drinking and drugs, but it does bear directly on them. It's the issue of *legality*. *The Christian is to obey the law*. The Bible is, if anything, even more explicit on this point than it is on drunkenness. Make a careful study of passages such as Romans 13, Titus 3, and I Peter 2 to see how tremendously important obedience to the law is in the New Testament view of things. It is not left to you to "make up your own mind" in this matter. Christian discipleship is, by definition, law-abiding.

There are important exceptions to this but they are of a very specific sort. The same apostle Peter who wrote, "submit yourselves, for the Lord's sake, to every human authority," (I Peter 2:13), also said, "We must obey God, not men" (Acts 5:29). Note, *you are to submit to legal human authority in all cases except those which would entail disobedience to God*. Thus, there is no such thing as the "right" to break a law. There is sometimes the *responsibility* to do so when that law contradicts the command of God. Because you do not like the law, or because you find it inconvenient, or you think it is silly, or you watch everybody else disregarding it are not adequate bases for your own disobedience to civil authority.

When Daniel was forbidden to worship God by the King of Persia, he broke the law in obedience to higher authority and took the consequences (Daniel 6). When Peter said he should obey God rather than men it was because the

Jewish authorities were trying to prohibit his preaching of the gospel. If certain laws in this country are racist and prejudicial, it's not your right, it's your responsibility, to oppose them and, if necessary, to break them.

However, if a law prohibits what you might otherwise like to do, but it is not in opposition to God's revealed will for us, you are to obey it—like it or not.

As we have said, while this goes far beyond liquor and drugs, it's implication here is obvious. The law says no pot, no other drugs, and no drinking for those who are "under age" (in most states twenty-one, in some, eighteen). The laws may be foolish, they may be excessive, they may be unnecessary, and they might be changed. Until they are changed we are to submit ourselves to them.

This is one of the many points at which discipleship to Christ may be costly. Every one of you has known how hard it is to resist "going along with the crowd." Anyone who has ever said "No" to peer pressure has felt the bitter sting of being called "chicken" and "out of it." At best, you're considered foolish. Mixed with the thrill of the illicit and the excitement of the forbidden is the smug satisfaction of knowing more than your parents, being able to laugh at the "Establishment." Illegality is never more compelling than when it masquerades under the name of "freedom."

True freedom, however, the freedom of the Christian, is the ability to withstand such pressures. You don't *need* these things if you belong to Christ. He will help you say "No" if you look to him for help. "If the Son makes you free, then you will be really free" (John 8:36). Taken together, the matters of *sobriety* and *legality* set firm boundaries for the Christian. You are not free to ignore them. But you are free to obey them. Heed what God says, and discover that his service is perfect freedom, his yoke easy, his burden light, and his fellowship worth all the cost of obedience (Matthew 11:30).

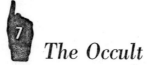

The Occult

In his famous poem, *Give All to Love,* Ralph Waldo Emerson suggested that "the half-gods go when God arrives." In this generation the truth of that statement is being reversed. As the power and influence of Christianity declines, that of the occult comes rushing back like the return of the sea. Beliefs and practices so long suppressed that most of our parents and grandparents thought them utterly groundless are finding new adherents among the young by the tens of thousands. "Parlor games" such as table-tapping and the ouija board, the reading of horoscopes, and the visiting of mediums—considered for centuries to be nothing more than harmless superstition—are suddenly being taken with the utmost seriousness. The practice of magic, witchcraft, and outright Satanism (worshipping the Devil) are once again major religious realities in the cultural experience of the West.

In a recent talk at Harvard University, Os Guiness pointed out that as jungle animals are driven into the wilderness when a campfire is well tended, but come creeping back if the fire should die out; so demonic and occult forces, driven out before the blazing truth of Christianity, have once again encircled us as its fire has all but died.[1] The time has come for Christians to rediscover that the occult is not nonsense; it is not neutral; it is not necessary.

It is not nonsense. C. S. Lewis once said that the Devil's favorite strategy is to make people think he doesn't exist.[2] Of late, the Church has been a great ally to him in this regard. Leading theologians and ministers during the last century have said that all the Biblical references to a world of supernatural evil are nothing more than metaphorical. They have regarded demon possession, for instance, as a pre-scientific way of referring to schizophrenia. They have said that charms, curses, and incantations work only on a psychological level—through the power of fear—and that the Devil is nothing more than the personification of human wrongdoing. Magic and witchcraft, seances and Satanism they have looked upon with contempt as subjects to become concerned with only when someone is superstitious enough to take them seriously. They have justified their disregard for the authority of the Scriptures by saying that the Bible was written in pre-scientific terms for a pre-scientific people and that it would not have been understood had it been written differently.

The argument against such skepticism is two-fold. First, there is the fact that Jesus and the Apostles dealt with the spiritual world supernaturally. It was not merely a matter of attitude, or a way of speaking about it, it was a matter of how they interacted with it. They spoke directly to demons, and *the demons spoke back*. They not only exercised authority over evil spirit, but Jesus promised that others who would follow—including you and me— would share such authority (Mark 16:17). To suggest that all this was merely a concession to the world-view of the time is to have an extremely low opinion of Jesus' own understanding of such things. He continually set himself over against the superstition of his age, denying, for instance, that blindness was the result of sin (John 9:3), or that ritual cleanliness could be of real moral significance (Mark 15:11). However, the belief in angels and demons he took as literally true and acted accordingly. Before setting his opinion aside you would do very well to recall his comment that "No pupil is greater than his teacher" (Luke 6:40).

Skepticism, however, is answered not only by Jesus' teaching; there is, also, the increasing prevalence of occult *experience* which speaks for itself. The late Bishop James Pike had come to the point where, though he remained a churchman, he virtually disbelieved in *all* supernaturalism (bad or good). He delivered one lecture in which he denied

the Virgin Birth, the miracles, the resurrection, the Second
Coming, and concluded by saying that Jesus was not essentially different from anybody else, he just used what powers
he had to better advantage. Shortly after this, Bishop Pike's
son committed suicide. Through a bizarre series of inexplicable events the Bishop and others began to question
whether it was possible that James Junior was trying to
contact them from "the other side." Clocks stopped, for no
discoverable reason, at precisely the hour of his death.
Books and postcards flew about the room, landing to form
the exact angle with each other that the hands of the clocks
formed. Strange, and frightening, experiences, such as that
of having their hair singed off during the night, began to
afflict members of the household. Finally, Bishop Pike
participated in a number of seances conducted by Arthur
Ford, a professional medium, through whom a voice other
than Ford's own spoke of things known only to the young
man and his father. The Episcopal skeptic was transformed
into a Spiritualist believer.

Thousands, perhaps millions, who scoff when they hear
of such phenomena second hand are being converted when
they encounter them personally.

All of this is not to deny the fact that the vast majority
of what purports to be occult is nothing more than fraud
and superstition. Rather it is to assert that every now and
then, something so powerful happens that reasonable, so-
phisticated people are forced to reverse previously held
skepticism.

The most conservative reports from England indicate
that over 30,000 men and women are practicing witchcraft
seriously. In this country, an estimated 5,000 astrologers
crank out horoscopes for over ten million Americans every
day, while who-knows-how-many follow the astrological
predictions in their daily newspapers. Law enforcement
agencies, high ranking officials of government, and even

Presidents of the United States have consulted psychics such as Peter Hurkos and Jeane Dixon for advice and counsel. It is not nonsense!

But, it is not neutral, either. In Deuteronomy 18, at the very outset of Israel's history, the lines were drawn with utmost clarity:

"There shall not be found among you any one . . . who practices divination [fortunetelling], or a soothsayer [astrology], or an augur [magician], or a sorcerer [witch], or a charmer [hypnotist], or a medium [one who allows an alien spirit or personality to 'guide' or speak through him], or a wizard [anyone who practices the black arts], or a necromancer [one who consults the dead]. For whoever does these things is an abomination to the Lord." (Deuteronomy 18:10-12 RSV)

Inserting the modern synonyms for each category brings that passage shockingly up-to-date, doesn't it? The Old Testament made all such practices punishable by death (Exodus 22:18, Leviticus 20:27), and the New Testament added that "those who do these things will not receive the Kingdom of God" (Galatians 5:19-21), they will not enter God's "city" (Revelation 22:14-15), but instead, "the place for them is the lake burning with fire and sulphur" (Revelation 21:8).

Not realizing this, or ignoring it, numbers of people who have seen so little of the miraculous for so long mistakenly reason that anything supernatural must be good. If God can heal, then every healing must come from God. If God has sent prophets, then every prophet must be divinely inspired. If miracles are real, they must surely originate in heaven. How different the view of Christ and the Scriptures! "False Messiahs and false prophets will appear," warned Jesus, "they will perform great signs and wonders ['miracles' in Greek] for the purpose of deceiving God's chosen people, if possible" (Matthew 24:24). Jesus said there would even be those who appear to do such things in his name who never really belonged to him at all (Matthew 7:23).

Why would Satan want to do something good, such as healing a person, if he is evil? Or, to put it another way, why should something which is itself good, a healing or a helpful prophesy, be condemned simply because it doesn't come from God? The answer is simple: Satan will use *anything* to ensnare and enslave human personalities. He is called, among other things, "a liar, and the father of all lies" (John 8:44). He masquerades as "an angel of light" (II Corinthians 11:14), mimicking the works of God, but hiding within them, like the barb in the bait, his insane desire to dominate and oppress. If healing someone's physical infirmity leads that person into spiritual bondage, he is delighted to perform the healing. Because bondage is precisely the goal he has in mind, the healing cannot be considered good because it cannot be considered by itself.

Too many people think that supernatural power is a neutral thing, good or bad depending upon how it is used. Thus they distinguish between "black" and "white" witchcraft and magic. "Black magic" is that which is used selfishly, that which harms others; "white magic" is used only altruistically to help people. That's similar to saying that because someone uses some of his money for charity it doesn't matter that he got it by graft, extortion, and murder! The Scriptures recognize no such distinction. Supernaural power that does not originate with God, and is not subservient to him, is of the Devil. Availing yourself of it— however "innocently"—is a matter of breaking the First Commandment and "having another god before God" (Exodus 20:3). Even the "mildest" forms of occult involvement such as having your palm read, or playing with the ouija board—more as a joke than anything else—is sin, however little you may realize it at the time. Just as with any other sin, it must be confessed and repented of, or its consequences may be great. Very deep psychological and spiritual oppression have been traced back to this particular type of sin since it was neither recognized nor treated as such. No, it is not neutral.

But neither is it necessary, praise God! Neither occult participation itself, nor the inevitable and devastating consequences need be a part of the Christian's life. It is, as we said in Chapter 3, God's pleasure to give his children all the guidance they request. There is no need to consult any other source of information no matter how pressing a problem you may ever face. "If any of you lacks wisdom, he should pray to God, who will give it to him; for God gives generously and graciously to all" (James 1:5). There is no need to turn elsewhere for healing: "Is there any one of you who is sick? He should call the church elders, who will pray for him and pour oil on him in the name of the Lord. This prayer, made in faith, will save the sick man: the Lord will restore him to health, and the sins he has committed will be forgiven" (James 5:14,15). While it is tragically true that we have seen far too little of this, one of the most exciting of all the promises of Scripture is that "When the enemy shall come in like a flood, the Spirit of the Lord shall lift up a standard against him" (Is 59:19 KJV). In the spring of 1970, magazine after magazine ran articles on the rise of occultism, the Black Arts, and Satanism—especially in California. A year later those same magazines were filled with articles on the "Jesus Movement" and the Christian Revolution sweeping the country— especially California. No healings? *Look* magazine reported over 4,000 kids sprung off of heroin addiction instantaneously by the power of Christ![3]

Even more important: while it's not necessary to turn to the power of the occult for any kind of help, neither is it necessary to remain in bondage to it if you have turned there in the past. "For I am certain that nothing can separate [those who have trusted in Christ] from his love: neither death nor life; neither angels nor other heavenly rulers or powers; neither the present nor the future; neither the world above nor the world below—there is nothing in all creation that will ever be able to separate us from the love of God which is ours through Christ Jesus our Lord" (Romans 8:38,39). Paul wrote that Christ rules "above all heavenly rulers, authorities, powers, and lords; he is above all titles of power in this world and in the next" (Ephesians 1:21); and, he said, that same power is in us (Ephesians 1:19)!

If you have had contact with this form of the Enemy's power, cast it out in the name of Christ. It is your right to do so (Mark 16:17). If your faith is not strong enough to do this alone, find a fellow Christian whose is. Have nothing more to do with it. It is an abomination to the Lord. Praise Jesus, for he is Victor, even—and especially—here. "Of course there's a Devil, but he's God's Devil"—Martin Luther.

NOTES

[1] "The Encircling Eyes: The Recent Resurgence of the Occult," March 9, 1971.

[2] *Cf.* Lewis, C. S., *The Screwtape Letters.* New York: The Macmillan Company, 1962, page 32.

[3] *Look,* March, 1971.

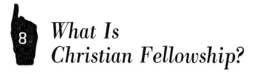

8   *What Is Christian Fellowship?*

IF YOU have ever tried to "go it alone" as a Christian, you know how important Christian fellowship is. There is nothing more wonderful than being with other Christians, sharing the marvellous things that God has been doing. Studying

God's word with those who share your exuberance for his truth is as exciting as any pursuit available to man. Praying for the needs of your brothers and sisters in Christ is a priceless opportunity to taste the satisfaction of helping others and being part of God's work. Having your friends pray for you is humbling and healing. The wonder of being accepted exactly as you are, by people who love you with that special love borne of a mutually shared secret, is to be found nowhere else on earth. It is God's way of bringing you into maturity as Christians. The surest way to make a shipwreck of your faith is to be without Christian fellowship week after week, month after month.[1] This chapter is intended to help you understand and appreciate Christian fellowship more deeply, know how to start a group if you do not have one, and begin to improve whatever group you have at the moment.

What it is:

Real Christian fellowship is a rare commodity. Too many Christian groups are handicapped by distrust, criticism, jealously, apathy, and an unwillingness on the part of most members to realize that they are one, in God's eyes, with every other member and should be acting that way. Take a long, hard look at your group, but before you do, examine your own heart for it will reveal to you the problems that must be overcome before genuine Christian fellowship can be enjoyed by you and your Christian friends.

Is there anyone in your group you are critical of? competing with? impatient with? Do you secretly wish that this one would keep his mouth shut, that one would lose a little weight, and all of them would pay a bit more attention to you? Multiply your uncharitable feelings by the number of Christians in your group and you can begin to understand why the quality of fellowship is lower than it might be.

Jesus said: "This is my commandment: love one another

as I love you" (John 15:12). That is the key to meaningful Christian fellowship. Jesus is not at this point telling us to love non-Christians, he is telling us to love the Christians that God has placed us with. How are we to love our Christian friends? The way Jesus loves us. That means with infinite patience, understanding, and acceptance, in spite of the faults, sins, and stupidity which we see in our friends.

The importance of this cannot be overemphasized. St. John said that our attitude towards our fellow Christians is the yardstick measuring our spiritual maturity. "He who says that he is in the light, yet hates his brother, is in the darkness to this very hour. He who loves his brother stays in the light, and he has nothing in himself that will cause someone else to sin" (I John 2:9). The word "brother" does not refer to our neighbor, it refers to fellow Christians. We cannot claim to be enlightened, to know God and walk with him, yet have chronic dislike for fellow Christians or any reluctance to be associated publicly with them[2] If you are in spiritual darkness because of a lack of love towards your fellow Christians, that darkness will cause other Christians to stumble and fall. The devil will certainly use any ill will in you to cause trouble and dissension in your group. "If we live in the light . . . then we have fellowship with one another and the blood of Jesus cleanses us from every sin" (I John 1:7). The way to powerful, Spirit-filled and love-saturated fellowship is for each member to live "in the light," bringing to God and relinquishing promptly any criticism towards other members of the group.

Why it's hard:

Although real Christian fellowship is the most supremely rewarding experience, it is also one of the most difficult to obtain. It is hard because loving is hard, and fighting is hard, and both are required.

It is a fight because non-Christians do not like to think

that some of their friends and acquaintances actually prefer Jesus Christ and his followers to their own company. Their hostility will find numerous, cruel ways of manifesting itself. If you have a strong Christian fellowship group, then you may have already experienced the sting of rebuke and criticism, the "God-Squad" label, the snide jeers behind your backs. Have you ever experienced the terrible pain and conflict of hearing a fellow Christian criticized, perhaps legitimately, by non-Christians? Did you side with your brother in Christ and defend him, sharing his shame? Or, did you in bewilderment and embarrassment join in slandering him or comply by saying nothing? You must always support your fellow Christians when they are under attack from outsiders for the reputation of Christ is at stake and your reaction is being closely watched. St. Paul praised the Philippian Christians for their unity towards the outside world: "I hear that you stand firm with one common purpose and fight together ... for the faith of the gospel. [Don't] be afraid of your enemies; [always be courageous,] and this will prove to them that they will lose and that you will win ... you have been given the privilege of serving Christ, not only by believing in him, but also by suffering for him" (Philippians 1:27-29). If your friends are under attack, defend them to their accusers. Later, in private conversation with those who were criticized, in a loving way investigate the truth of the charges. It is not an easy thing to let the world's hatred of Christ fall on you or on your friends. It is a battle of the highest order for behind it is the devil, seeking to discredit Christians and disrupt their unity. St. Paul says it is a *privilege* to suffer thus.

Real Christian fellowship is hard because there is still so much in you that is proud and stiffnecked, that rebels at serving others. St. Paul wrote: "be humble toward each other, never thinking you are better than others. Look out for each other's interests, not for your own. . . . The atti-

tude you should have is the one that Christ Jesus had . . .
he took the nature of a servant . . . he was humble and
walked the paths of obedience" (Philippians 2:3-8). You
cannot be like Jesus in isolation. Only by trying to live in
close, devoted contact with other Christians will you have
the opportunity to become mature sons of God. Real Christian unity involves yielding yourself to the group, and living as an example to every other member. You must permit some of your rough edges to be worn smooth through
the tension of group interaction. You must learn patience
by submitting yourself to people who drive you nuts. You
must learn humility by receiving instruction from those you
think are less mature than you. If you hunger for greatness in the kingdom of God, the way to find it is through
the humiliation of serving other Christians. That is the way
Jesus took, and the servant is not greater than his master.

How to get a fellowship group going:

If you are all alone without Christian fellowship, you
know how precious it is. You are in a difficult and precar-
ious position, but there are some things you might try.

Until you can get a group of your own started, try to
find a church fellowship group for young people. If you
are unhappy with your own parish (and it would not upset
your parents too much), ask God to help you find one where
the minister stresses the Bible and a personal relationship
with Jesus Christ. A youth group in such a parish is likely
to enjoy a lively spiritual fellowship. If you are unable to
get there on your own, call the church and ask the minister
if he has any parishioners from your neighborhood who
might be willing to pick you up on Sundays. Most church-
goers would be delighted to give a young person a ride to
and from their church.

If you want to start a group of your own, you must have
other young Christians to help you. Ask God to lead you to

fellow students at your school who know him, or who are open to belief in him. Be bold enough to initiate conversations with them about Christ and if they nibble, pursue it. You may be privileged to lead them into commitment to Christ. If you can find (or produce) only one other Christian, you have the beginning of a group. Meet regularly, share what God is doing in your lives, and pray together. Each time you pray, ask God to lead you to others and he will. If you are personally faithful, patient, and persistent, considering this a top priority item in your prayers, God will bring a fellowship group into being around you. Just don't be too picky about those he brings!

What to do during meetings:

First, you will have to meet regularly at a time when you can all get together. Then, finding a place might be a real challenge for the Holy Spirit, and there may have to be some sacrifices if you are to find a time suitable to everyone. Third, once you have a time and place, the greatest problem will be getting the conversation to center around God. Fourth, there should be a definite time when the meeting begins and ends, and, fifth, to make sure it does not degenerate into social chit-chat, a leader should be selected for each meeting, someone capable of arresting the pre-meeting conversations and bringing everyone's attention to the Lord.[3]

Just being together, talking trivia, is not Christian fellowship. Your meetings can be highly structured, with a definite program followed regularly at each meeting; or they can be quite loose, permitting each member to share, pray, suggest a song, share a spiritual gift, or read a Bible passage. We might suggest that every meeting should include a brief study of scripture, a limited time for personal sharing, and a time for specific, vocal prayer. This may seem too binding to some, but Christian fellowships that

stray from the basic forms of instruction, praise, and prayer
soon fail altogether. Folk songs, hymn-singing, periods of
silent meditation, prayers for healing, special guest speak-
ers might all be included from time to time. However your
group functions, try to begin and end on time. Make a
concerted effort to discourage small private conversations
during the meeting, moving in and out of the room to get
refreshments while the meeting is in progress, and interruptions from telephone or curious family members.

Some Christians feel uncomfortable praying or sharing in
the presence of non-Christians. If there are members of your
group who feel this way, you could have two different
meetings, one for Christians only (never publicized) and
another, less frequent perhaps, where Christians are encouraged to bring their non-Christian friends. At such a
meeting, you should probably not include specific prayer
for people who are not present. The non-Christian guests
might know the individuals being prayed for and interpret
your praying as gossip or meddling. While non-Christians
tend to enjoy meetings where there is a good deal of spontaneous sharing, it is unwise to reveal deeply personal problems. An interesting speaker or Bible study presenting some
basic aspect of the gospel and an opportunity for questions
is a sound format for the main feature. Since it is your
responsibility to arouse interest and hunger for God, not to
stimulate unhealthy curiosity or embarrass people, be
somewhat careful about manifesting gifts of the Spirit or
displaying excessive emotion. The Christians present should
make a great effort to get to know the non-Christians and
if someone comes to several meetings be sure to find out
exactly where that person is spirtually. A girl came to the
meetings of a fellowship group for several months and
then ceased abruptly. One day a member asked her why she
had stopped coming. "Well, no one seemed to care what I
was thinking, and I just wasn't brave enough to start asking

religious questions," she replied. Try to overcome your natural reluctance to talk personally with semi-strangers and find out where those who come to your meetings are in their spiritual search. If you can't answer their questions, try to find someone who can.

If asked "What is the most effective way to win others to Christ?" some of you would reply "by sharing the gospel message with them." Others might add "by living a righteous, joyous life." But Jesus said this: "I pray that they may all be one . . . so that the world will believe that you sent me" (John 17:20-23). Surprised? The one thing that will convince the world that Jesus is the son of God is to show that you and your Christian friends love each other with such passion and purity that you are, indeed, "one." Everyone in the world is eager for acceptance, love, and support from others. If Christians display real love, refusing to criticize each other, preferring each other's company, sharing honestly and deeply, experiencing the presence of the Spirit of God in their midst as they humbly and earnestly seek to please him in their meetings, the world will realize that they have something extraordinary, something from God. Non-Christians who are truly seeking Life will find their spirtual mouths watering when they observe the love and joy you share together "If you have love for one another, then all will know that you are my disciples," Jesus said (John 13:35). What is the greatest Christian witness? A love-filled fellowship.

As the world becomes increasingly hostile to Christianity, it will be harder—yet more necessary—for you to spend time in Christian fellowship. If there is any resistance in you, relinquish it right now. If you have a fellowship group, begin to ask God to show you how you might be a better member of it. One day we will all be caught up together as Christ's Bride, and that glorious calling is only for those who have proven here and now their eagerness to function as one with their brothers and sisters in the Lord.

NOTES

[1] "Let us not give up the habit of meeting together." Hebrews 10:25

[2] The exception to this is found in I Corinthians 5:11, "... you should not associate with a man who calls himself a brother but is immoral, or greedy, or worships idols, or is a slanderer, or a drunkard, or a law-breaker. Don't even sit down to eat with such a person."

[3] A well-proven method for doing this is to get everyone's attention and ask: "Well, what has the Lord been doing in your lives? What have you been learning from him?" Or, "Does anyone have anything he'd like to share about what God is doing in his life?" A few moments of silence may ensue. However, that won't hurt anyone. Be prepared to speak if you are the leader, waiting to make sure that others are not going to speak first.

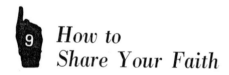

9 How to Share Your Faith

WHEN PEOPLE meet the Living God in a personal way, when their lives are changed by him, their immediate response is to tell others about it. Yet, for a great many Christians, something seems to happen after the initial flush of enthusiasm. They begin to be self-conscious about their faith. They feel awkward about speaking of it. Sometimes, of course, this is because of a problem in their relationship with God himself: unconfessed sin or inattentiveness to his Word or to prayer will make them feel hypocritical in telling others how wonderful knowing God is. More often, the problem is simply that new Christians don't know quite what to say, and they don't know how to say it.

In New Testament language, speaking to others about Christ is a matter of "witnessing." The last recorded words of Jesus were: "You will be witnesses for me in Jerusalem, in all of Judea and Samaria, and to the ends of the earth" (Acts 1:8).

Not understanding what this means is a major part of the hang-up in the business of sharing the faith. Witnessing does not necessarily mean talking theology. It does not have to involve walking up to strangers and asking them if they know Jesus, or passing out tracts to everyone you see. While God does equip some people to minister very effectively along these lines, most of us are not able to master theology or our own natural shyness sufficiently to witness in these ways.

Witnessing in the most basic Christian sense is very similar to witnessing in the legal sense. A witness is simply an individual who tries to recount with accuracy what he has seen, heard, and (where relevant) felt. Witnessing is *sharing your own personal, "eyewitness" experience.*

The New Testament makes it very clear that while not all are called to be preachers (though some are) and not all are called to be evangelists (though some are), all are asked to be witnesses: to be involved in telling others what God has done in their lives. Peter wrote: "Be ready at all times to answer anyone who asks you to explain the hope you have in you" (I Peter 3:15). (Note the assumption that our "hope" will be so evident it will cause people to inquire about it!) Jesus put it very strongly when he said, "Whoever confesses publicly that he belongs to me, I will do the same for him before my Father in heaven. But whoever denies publicly that he belongs to me, then I will deny him before my Father in Heaven" (Matthew 10:32-33).

Witnessing is not optional, it's part of being a follower of Jesus, but neither is it difficult—at least, it shouldn't be. It is a matter of sharing, simply, honestly, and lovingly what has happened to you.

Forgetting this leads to problems. You know perfectly

well that you cannot answer all of the philosophical arguments that people may throw at you, so admit it! Part of witnessing is the honest "I don't know" when you don't. This doesn't mean that you shouldn't try to find out (the whole latter part of this book is designed to help you) or that you shouldn't share your findings; it does mean that the major task of the witness is to say, "I know that God is real because he has made himself real to me. He will make himself real to you, too, if you want him to."

The ability to say this simply and naturally comes with practice. It begins with the honest willingness to *try*. What *has* happened to you? What *do* you know to be true?

The witness who relies on hearsay evidence, or on his own opinion, is thrown out of court. Don't talk about what you think *should* have happened to you or about what you think the other person *needs* to hear. Talk about what you know from knowing God personally. If that isn't very much, don't worry about it. Has God become a real Person to you? Share that. Can you perhaps put into words what you felt and thought at the time he entered your life (you might practice this when you are alone)? Is it important to you that all your sins and mistakes are forgiven because you trust in Christ? Share *that* with your friend. The chances are that he or she is eager to know the same sort of forgiveness (even though he or she might not admit it to you right now). Has God answered prayer? Tell your friend about that—it will give him hope. Has God guided you in some important matter? Has he blessed you with a new sense of peace, security, freedom since you became a Christian? Has he helped you handle a difficult personal relationship? Sharing any of these things is witnessing because it is telling, simply, what you have learned through personal experience with God. Be yourself, and your natural enthusiasm for Jesus will lead you to tell others about what he has done for you.

There is another major reason, however, why people sometimes have trouble witnessing. That is, they discover that some of their friends (and sometimes members of their families) are hostile to Christianity. Jesus warned his disciples over and over that they would suffer the same rejection he suffered in a world that crucified him. In fact, he said that the more closely you identify with him and his purposes, the more likely it is that you will be treated as he was (See John 15:18-27). Often, one of the greatest problems a teenager faces is relating to his parents who don't understand what he means when he says he has *become* a Christian (we'll discuss this in the next chapter). Wasn't he that before? Hadn't they always sent him to Sunday School? Wasn't theirs a Christian home?

Both parents and friends may call you "holier than thou" as you try to share your new faith with them. They will throw every mistake back at you: "I thought you were supposed to be such a great Christian—you can't even make your bed in the morning without being told to!" You must be very careful not to make your new faith sound like an announcement that you have *arrived* spirtually and morally.

Criticism and even ridicule may come anyway, no matter how circumspect your conduct. There is nothing that will make this easy except to realize that you are sharing in Christ's sufferings because you also share a portion of his love. St. Paul said that by sharing Christ's sufferings we are made like him (Philippians 3:10), and he exhorted his young friend Timothy to "take your part in suffering, as a loyal soldier of Christ Jesus" (II Timothy 2:3).

Therefore, the real answer to the question of *how* to witness is not a matter of what formula to use, but what attitude to adopt. Witness lovingly and patiently. Jesus said that men would recognize his disciples by the quality of their love (John 13:35). Our words are crucial but unless they are expressed in love nobody will be able to hear them.

Paul said, "it is love that you should strive for" (I Corinthians 14:1). Are you doing that? If not, all the good theology in the world will be little better than blasphemy because it will be "taking the Lord's name in vain."

Have you ever thought about what it means to be really loving? loving the way Jesus was loving? Loving is much more than making your bed in the morning without being asked to, more than helping your mother set the table without grumbling, more than refraining from arguing with your kid brother or sister when he or she becomes obnoxious.

What about the lonely, unpopular kid who has a locker near you but who never has any friends clustering about after school? Love risks social status by befriending the friendless and loving the unlovely. How is anyone going to believe that your God cares for him when *you don't?* Is there anything sacrificial, costly, about your love? Are there any acts of real compassion in your life based not on mutual admiration but on discernment of the needs of others? Do you ever act without regard for your own needs or popularity? Everybody tries to *appear* loving and kind; everybody loves the people he likes! It takes more than a superficial friendliness to be a witness to the love and power of Christ. If men are to identify you as a disciple *by your love* you had better concentrate on a caliber of love which far exceeds the for-appearances-only brand you see all around you.

If you are really striving after love, most of the problems in relating to people, especially those involved in sharing your faith with them, work themselves out (or, more accurately, *God* works them out!) (See Philippians 2:12, 13). How much do you say in witnessing? As much as love allows. When the other person has had enough for one time, he will let you know it by changing the subject. If love is your aim, you will be sensitive to this. Love will show you when to stop just as it will show you how to begin. A friend has a problem—in love, you might be able to say quite naturally, "have you ever thought about trusting God with your problem?" As the conversation unfolds you may be able to share not only the fact that God can help out with a particular problem, but also that he can change whole lives. Or, you may be able to begin something that you can come back to later as God prepares your friend to hear more from you—in love.

"Results" are God's business!

If there is anything you must never do, it is to try to produce a spiritual experience in anybody. The early disciples told people about Jesus, prayed for them, answered their questions to the best of their ability, and left the results up to the Holy Spirit. This is the only permissible pattern.

Occasionally, God will use your witness to bring a person right up to the point of conversion. Love will enable you to see that it is appropriate to ask, "do you want to give your life to Christ right now?" Don't feel you need to press for this, however. Don't even suggest it unless you have a strong sense that it would be the right time. *God* will bring that person to him in his own time and your witness may be just one of many steps along the path. Wrenching the matter out of God's hands is sure to produce an abortion rather than a new birth!

Remember, your witness is the appetizer. The main course is the gospel itself. Chapter 15 may help you in articulating its content. People begin to become excited about God's reality by seeing that reality in someone's life; they become converted by hearing about what Christ did for them 2,000 years ago. The purpose of witnessing is to make others hungry for more. Don't try to convert anyone to your experience! Share it, and if your friend then "asks for an answer for the hope that is within you," "be ready" to explain Christ's death and resurrection, his promise of forgiveness, and his offer of new life.

God wants you to be yourself. Only as you relax in his love and dare to be the free, happy, unselfconscious person he created you to be, will you be an effective witness. You needn't memorize spiritual laws, study methods of evangelism, or plan strategies. As you drop all affections, all phoniness, all role-playing, and forget about the impression you might be creating, God's love in you will have a chance to get through to your friend. Try forgetting about yourself, and think about helping others discover the wonderful God you have found. Have fun in your faith! The Lord is with you, and, if you will allow the spontaneous joy he's given you to radiate through you as you speak of him, your words will have a convincing ring of truth no matter how inadequate they may sound to you.

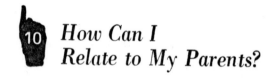

10 *How Can I Relate to My Parents?*

CHARLIE CAME to see us the other day. His words tumbled out, "I've just about had it with my parents. I love them and all that—and I know they love me—but we just don't get along. They're always checking up on me like they don't trust me. And when I don't do something the moment they tell me to they start in with what a rotten Christian I am. . . ."

"Hold it!" I interrupted. "*Are* you a rotten Christian? Why *don't* you do things the minute your parents ask you to? Or even before they ask? If they are always checking up on you, is it because you haven't ever really proven to them that they *can* trust you? You say you know they love you, but *do they know you love them?* When was the last time you said so? The last time you showed it?"

"Hey, how come you're siding with them?"

I wasn't siding with them; neither was I suggesting that all the fault was on Charlie's side. I was saying, however, that Charlie's side was the only one he could do much about.

This realization is the key to *all* of your relationships from the New Testament point of view. Others may have responsibilities to you, and it may be that they are not carrying them out as well as they should (or as well as you *think* they should). However, that's between them and God. Your responsibilities toward them are not on an "I'll meet you half-way" basis. You are to go all the way in meeting your responsibilities—even if they go none of the way in meeting theirs.

If I were writing to parents I would have a good deal to say about God's instructions to parents. I'm not, however. I'm writing to you and God's instructions to you are the same as his instructions to Charlie: "Honor your parents." No qualifications. No hidden clauses. Nothing whatsoever about honoring your parents *if* they're the sort of parents you think they should be; *if* they're Christians; *if* they allow you all the freedom you think you deserve; *if*; *if*; *if*. . . . No, God leaves no such bargaining room. He states it simply, as one of his ten most basic rules,

"Honor your father and your mother, that your days may be long in the land which the Lord your God gives you." (Exodus 20:12 RSV)

That sounds, at first, as harsh and unsympathetic as did my response to Charlie's complaint. However, I think that's because there are no less than four very important things that most people overlook completely with regard to it.

First, it's not addressed to little children; it's addressed to children who have grown up (or who are well along the way toward doing so); to children who may already be adults, but who still are children in relationship to their parents.

How do I know this? Well, think for a moment about the society to which this commandment was originally given. The father was king in his own family. His word was law. He could be arbitrary, selfish, perverse. He could sell his children into slavery if he was in debt and could find no better way to pay his bills. His will was absolute; his children had no higher court of appeal. For a little child in ancient Israel "honor your father and your mother" was about as superfluous as "thou shalt breathe."

However, once a man took a wife and left his father and mother, his relationship to them changed completely. Suddenly *he* was king of his own castle, and his parents, all too often, were forgotten and abandoned. One of the shocking brutalities of the day was the expulsion of the aged from society—to die by exposure or from the attack of wild beasts (a practice still carried on in parts of the world today).

Then came the commandment: *honor* your parents when they've long since lost their financial usefulness. Civilization took a mighty leap forward!

Do you see the implication of this? *Honoring* begins where *obligation* leaves off. Whereas obligation is compulsory, honoring is voluntary. Thus, the ability truly to honor your parents is something you grow into, not something you grow out of.

Secondly, if honoring is not obligation, neither is it obedience. The commandment doesn't mention obedience, it talks about honor. Little children, of course, must obey their parents (and St. Paul tells them to do so—Ephesians 6:1; Colossians 3:20); if they don't they will be punished.

Adult children, however, are under no such compulsion.

In fact, it is only as you outgrow the requirements of obedience that you can begin to honor.

The problem in growing up is that you are changing far more than your parents. You do outgrow the patterns of childhood, but if you find nothing to replace them, your parents will probably expect you to fit into them long after you have stopped doing so comfortably. Every boy gets to the point where he no longer wants to kiss his father goodnight. What alternative way will he find of saying "I love you?" Up to a certain point it makes sense for a girl to be in from a date at 10 o'clock and "tell Mom all about it." When it no longer makes sense, how will she continue to assure her mother that her need for privacy isn't a rejection of the mother herself? If you outgrow the childhood patterns and find nothing to replace them your parents will feel threatened, and neglected. They will feel they are losing their children and rather than permit that they will demand that you act as you have always acted—to prove you still love them.

I asked Charlie when he had last taken his parents out to dinner. He admitted that he had never even thought of it and he did it that weekend. It was a simple thing, but it marked a turning point. Here was an *adult* way for a child to say "I love you" to his parents.

Saying "I love you" is critically important when it comes to the matter of sharing your faith with your parents. Unless you are very careful, "I've become a Christian!" seems to say "I never was a Christian. The upbringing you gave me, the Sunday School you sent me to, the Church we attend together—all these have failed. Now, without any help from you, I've found the truth!" And even worse, the implication is "You haven't." (Maybe they *haven't,* but who are you to say so? That's between them and God.)

How much better to begin by thanking them for whatever help they gave you! "You know, Dad, I never cared much for Sunday School, but I'm beginning to see what it was about all along. I'm so grateful to you and Mom for starting me off in the right direction. Christ is really becoming real to me. . . ."

It may be that they didn't give you much of a start. It may be that no matter how careful you are they are antagonistic to your faith. No matter—love them anyway. Honor your father and your mother. Pray for them. Include them in your experience *as they ask to be included* (I Peter 3:15) and it may be that in his own time God will use you to bring them to a knowledge of himself. In any event *you* will learn more about his love than in any other way possible.

So—honoring is not obligation, and it's more than obedience. Let's press that further for a third point: it is possible that your parents would demand of you certain things that you must *not* do. Your relationship to your parents is somewhat like your relationship to the State. You should try to comply with their wishes up to the point where they demand of you something that Christ forbids, or prohibit something he requires. In the matter of choosing a career, for instance, or a marriage partner, you must look to God for direction, not to your parents' aspirations for you.

A friend of ours had planned to "follow in his father's footsteps" and become an engineer. To his family's great delight he won a scholarship. Then came the Spirit's urging to enter the ministry. The family thought he had become a fanatic, that he was wasting his life, but they couldn't dissuade him and the tensions ran deep. Years later, in the midst of a family crisis, those parents reached out to God and thanked their son for the example he had set for them. Today, the father is studying for the ministry —and his son is tutoring him!

Honoring, then, is not obligation, it's not (necessarily) obedience, and it's not living up to your parents' expectations. What *is* it? A dictionary would say that to honor is to "regard with high public esteem." It's a matter of taking pride and delight in two other people to whom you are indebted more deeply than you could ever repay, and acknowledging them as such in the company of your (other) friends.

Finally, notice that of all the Ten Commandments this is the only one with a *promise* attached to it. "Honor your parents *that your days may be long. . . .*" There's nothing magical about this. It's a piece of straightforward practical advice. You may remember the parable of the little old man who lived with his married son and daughter-in-law. His hands trembled, he had trouble eating, and usually he spilled things. So, they made him a little table out in back. When one day they noticed their own son playing with some bits of wood, they asked what he was doing. He replied, "I'm making a little table to feed you at when I get big."

Becoming the sort of parent whose children find him honorable begins with being the sort of child who honors his parents.

You may not be able to solve all of the problems of the Generation Gap alone. Begin by bridging the part of it that is a gap between your desire to be treated like an adult and your failure to act like one. You do your part, without worrying about your parents' part, and they may end up surprising you even more than you surprise them.

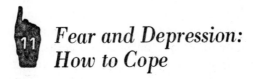

Fear and Depression: How to Cope

NOT EVERYONE struggles with fear and depression. For some, fear is only an occasional, momentary thing. For others, however, it can be a chronic, wearisome burden. St. John promises that "perfect love [that is, Christ's love] drives out all fear" (I John 4:18). This chapter is intended only for those who haven't yet been able to enter into the fulfillment of that promise; for those still hampered by fears, anxiety, depression, negativism, self-doubt—the whole bundle of emotional despair that can paralyze you spiritually, ruin your witness to others, and make you incapable of normal social relations. If this is not your problem, thank God it isn't, and skip this chapter. It's not really rated "G.P." anyway.

For some of you, it comes as a crushing disappointment to discover that Christians are not immune to fear, anxiety, depression, and like emotions. It should be encouraging to you to know that these "valleys" are not God's will for you. God's standard for his children is joy, spontaneity, and unself-consciousness, not the numb anguish of a bound spirit. Emotional problems are not overcome in a day although God's word recognizes that they exist and offers sound, workable advice for those who are trying to find release so they may serve God better.

When John the Baptist was born, his father Zachariah burst into a prophecy concerning the Messiah. One of the Christ's purposes, he said, was to enable man "to serve God without fear" (Luke 1:74). Many people are still a bit nervous about God, secretly suspecting that he is going to hurt them in order to "teach" them or make them good. Are you skeptical about God's character or motives, at least so far as they pertain to you? Then, you are thinking about a god quite different from the God Jesus knew and revealed. God sent his Son for the express purpose of helping confused, fearful people, like you and me, know exactly what he is really like so that you needn't be afraid anymore. God is like Jesus: gentle, patient, accepting, always ready to understand, to heal, to encourage. God's intentions for you are the highest: that you might be happy and free, productive, and sensitive. God loves you without qualification and he loved you like that long before you dreamed of returning his love. Nothing will happen to you that he does not permit and oversee and everything he allows in your life is only an opportunity for you to discover his love more vividly. Do you fear that he will let terrible things happen to you? Then rejoice, for he will take special care to prove you wrong.

Fear is usually the result of your failing to take the God of Jesus into account as you contemplate real or imagined dangers to yourselves, your loved ones, or your treasures. You need to begin controlling your imagination, refusing to ponder the troubles and failures you have already experienced or are (you think) likely to experience in the future. Every thought, imagining, and feeling must be brought into subjection to Jesus Christ (II Corinthians 10:5). The only moment that requires your attention is *now*. Put the future in God's hands and refuse to fret about it. God will be in your tomorrows just as he is in your todays.

It is easier to say that than it is to act on it. Fears and anxieties can only be overthrown by an active effort on your part, by a deliberate refusal to worry, and by placing your concerns into God's hands and leaving them there. You must will yourself to trust and shut your mind to the haunting cries of fear. As you trust God and his word and diligently resist the fears, they will begin to subside. Here are some of the things that the Bible has to say about handling fear:

"When I am afraid, I will trust in thee, in God, whose word I praise" (Psalm 56:4 RSV). Where should your attention be when you are afraid? On God and his word. Read it; believe it; cling to it. Learn to substitute reality (God's truth) for the lies you have been believing. Praise him!

Even if you don't feel like it, make yourself praise God. It is truly astonishing how rapidly words of praise, even timid ones, can put to flight the vultures of fear and anxiety.

"God is our refuge and strength, a very present help in trouble. Therefore we will not fear, though the earth be removed" (Psalm 46:1 KJV). What's a refuge? It is a safe, secure place to run when your enemies are after you. Are you besieged? Run to the Lord! Is your "earth" about to be "removed"? Fearing will not alter that fact, but the Lord of heaven and earth is available and he can handle anything you care to give him. You haven't the strength to cope with the things that happen to you, but *he* does—and immediately available strength, at that! If you run to him, confident that he can meet your needs, you will not be disappointed.

"With the Lord on my side, I do not fear. What can man do to me?" (Psalm 118:6 RSV). Think about that one. Almighty God is on *your* side! What enemies could possibly overcome you with the Lord on your side? Stop arguing with the truth—believe it! Are you afraid of what people may say about you or do to you? God won't let them do a thing to you that he knows you can't handle. A Christian life isn't an easy one; there are always hurdles to leap, obstacles to overcome, and the rejection of men to cope with. If your attitude is one of defeat and fright, these will appear far worse than they really are. If you keep your eyes on the living God, they will appear quite conquerable.

All of these passages stress one thing: your own will power. You may know theoretically that God is good and loves you; you must *act* on that knowledge if it is to make any difference in your life. You must wrench your will out of fear's grip and determine not to let it dominate you any more. "I *will* praise." "I *will not* fear." Those are statements from an aroused, determined soul. Fight your fear by concentrating on God instead of on the things you fear. That's not easy, for there is an evil allure about all those problems, but you can do it. Jesus said "fear not," and "be not anxious" (Matthew 6:25-34). Those are not suggestions, they are commands. He would not have given them if they were impossible. God won't strip you of your fear; you gave in to it in the first place, you are the one who must kick it out.

Depression comes in all shape and sizes and can be caused by many things. The most important thing that can be said to a person who is susceptible to depression is: "Don't allow yourself a moment's indulgence in self-pity, criticism, moodiness, restlessness. These can blossom into full-fledged depression overnight if they are not curbed immediately. The surest preventive medicine is daily (better yet, twice daily) times of prayer and Bible reading when you bring to God every sinful attitude, thought or action that has tried to dominate you and relinquish it to him. If you walk closely with God, keeping constant check on your moods, hiding nothing, your spirit will not become depressed and 'down.' "

There are ways of overcoming depression once it has gripped you, if you truly want to be free of it. Sometimes we say we do, but we secretly enjoy depression. You can begin by asking God's Spirit to help you trace your depression to its root cause. Is there any sin or wrong you have done which you have not confessed? Hidden sin can fester unnoticed for a long time and result in serious depression. Be willing to go back many years if necessary. Be honest about your own responsibility for the sin; do not place blame on others. Their fault is not your problem. Make restitution if you have hurt anyone. Confession to a minister or older Christian can often help you feel sure of God's forgiveness, but only if you are truly honest and are not seeking their sympathy or support for your efforts to avoid full responsibility for what you have done.

The Spirit might bring to light a relationship or experience which has hurt you badly. Wrongs done to you can affect you as seriously as the wrongs you do to others. Perhaps, someone close to you has wounded you deeply with a rebuke, a criticism, a slight, or through a misunderstanding. Perhaps, you were involved in some shocking experience, some upheaval which you have never fully faced, accepted, and given to God. Forgive those who have hurt you—including God if you are blaming him for something. Place the unhappy incident in God's hand; trust him to heal its effects even though many years may lie between its occurrence and the moment you yield it to God for healing. Time means nothing to God. The healing of memories is a gift from the Holy Spirit for those of us who live in a difficult, tension-strewn age.

St. Paul once said "we are not fighting against human beings, but against wicked spiritual forces in the heavenly world" (Ephesians 6:12). Depression, like fear, can be caused by demonic powers. Isaiah speaks of a "spirit of heaviness" (Isaiah 61:3 KJV) which may well refer to the oppressive activity of an evil spirit. God's word assures you, however, that if you "resist the devil he will flee from you" (James 4:7 KJV).

Past contact with the occult in any form (ouija, tarot, automatic writing, fortune telling, seances) is frequently associated with a sense of unreality about God and an increase in apathy and depression. If you have practiced any of the black arts you may have become the target of oppressive demons. To get rid of them you must admit that your occult activity was sinful (Deuteronomy 18:9-14), confess it to God, and then renounce it. A simple prayer of renunciation might be: "In the name of Jesus Christ I renounce any evil spirit which has found access into my life through my occult activity (be specific) and command you to go and never return. I claim by faith the cleansing of Christ's blood for this sin. Amen." Numbers of people who have found no release through psychological therapy or other channels have been astonished by the healing that results when such confession is made. Even those quite skeptical that there could be a connection between occult involvement and later depression have been dramatically liberated when, on the authority of God's word, they have confessed as sin what they previously regarded as nothing but superstition.

Your physical condition can also make a profound difference in your mental and spiritual outlook. Medical science has evidence that low blood sugar, for example, or an undetected case of mononucleosis, can cause emotional tension and depression. Try to eat more sensibly, reduce your intake of sweets and caffeine, get more sleep, and exercise regularly. Athletic activity is wonderfully helpful, providing you refuse to fall back into your depression-thoughts once you are off the playing field. Of course, it is imperative that you avoid all drugs, including marijuana and alcoholic beverages.

There are things you should *not* do if you are depressed. The most important is this: You must not imagine that you have any right to indulge in depression when you are capable of overthrowing it. It brings shame on the name of Christ; it is choosing darkness over light; it is preferring lies to truth, bondage to freedom. You *must* fight the moods that dominate you, no matter how justified or even pleasant they may seem. To help you fight them, don't introspect. That's a tough one because introspection is the great compulsion of the depressed personality. Resist it by keeping as busy as possible and attentive to what you are doing as you are doing it. Don't talk about your inner turmoil. Don't focus on your helplessness or the amount of work you have to do and can't. Do one thing at a time: do it for the Lord if you can't find any other motivation capable of energizing you. Reject any thoughts of withdrawal or suicide. You must begin your battle with small skirmishes. Victory in one area, however small, will make the next mountain less difficult to conquer.

Depression and fear are seldom permanent conditions, so cheer up. In his first epistle Peter suggests that such trials are not uncommon and are permitted to occur so that we might emerge stronger in faith for having mastered them (I Peter 1:6 KJV especially). "Lift up your limp hands, then, and strengthen your weak knees!" (Hebrews 12:12). Do not be distraught. Take heart; God is greater than your fear, your anxiety, your depression. Even the devil belongs to God after all. You are greatly loved by the One to whom nothing is impossible if you will only seek him and believe.

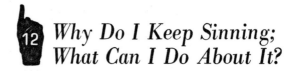

12 *Why Do I Keep Sinning; What Can I Do About It?*

"I THOUGHT God changed your life when you became a Christian. Well, I can't see that he's changed mine very much. I just can't live the way God wants me to. I don't know whether to be mad at him, or mad at me. Why is it so hard, now that I'm a Christian, to live like one?"

You became a Christian and the whole world looked different—cleaner, brighter. You felt different inside, full of love for God and delight in his love for you. Then, a day, a week, a month later, you found yourself doing exactly the same things you used to do, only now they seem worse because you'd hoped for so much more. Doesn't Christ make a difference? Hasn't God changed your life?

Does this failure mean you're not really committed to him? Is there any way to stop sinning so much?

Such questions race through the mind of every Christian who has ever taken seriously Christ's call to righteous living. The words above were written by a fourteen-year-old; you can find an almost perfect parallel to them, written by St. Paul, in Romans 7. None of us escapes the crushing blow of discovering that we're *still* sinners.

Why does the Christian keep sinning? Because he has not yet learned the nature of his new life and how to wage war effectively against the power of sin. According to St. Paul, the Christian is a person composed of two selves, two natures, the old one and the new one. The old one is used to running the show; it strives for its own rights, dominance over others, the approval of the world, the accumulation of possessions, and, generally speaking, the right to do whatever it wants, whenever it wants, however it wants. The new self, on the other hand, is the self that came into being when a person's will and the Spirit of God were joined together as that person yielded his life to Jesus Christ. That nature, that self, yearns only to please and delight God, and it is appalled when the old nature cons the Christian into sin. St. Paul says this: I don't do what I would like to do, but instead I do what I hate . . . But I am not really the one who does this thing; rather it is the sin that lives in me (Romans 7:17-20). That's encouraging, because it explains the whole business and makes one thing very clear: the real self, the self that matters, is not the self that initiates and delights in sin.

But, what do you do with this peculiar duality? Paul goes on to say "Sin must no longer rule in your mortal bodies, so that you obey the desires of your natural self. Nor must you surrender any part of yourself to sin, to be used for wicked purposes" (Romans 6:12-13). Pretty straightforward—you've got the job of resisting the old nature, using your transformed will to force your body, mind, and emotions to serve God rather than the old nature. Your Christ-centered self must dominate your old nature with its fears, its defensiveness, its need to be right, and powerful, and secure in this world. Praise God, it is possible. Hannah White-hall Smith describes the battle in this way:

The will is like a wise mother in a nursery; the feelings are like a set of clamoring, crying children. The mother makes up her mind to a certain course of action which she believes to be right and best. The children clamor against it and declare it shall not be. But the mother, knowing that she is mistress and not they, pursues her course lovingly and calmly in spite of all their clamors; and the result is that the children are sooner or later won over to the mother's course of action and fall in with her decisions.[1]

If only Christians could realize that the new self is to be lord and sovereign over the old nature, and begin refusing to let the old self have its way.

How, in practice, does the Christian go about affirming the new nature and rejecting the old nature? It works like this: the moment you realize that you are sinning, you must stop. Let it go. Yes, it's that simple—and that painful. Your old nature will whine and cry and beg you to continue in your resentment, your lying, your anger, your self-pity, your immorality, whatever it is that has gotten hold of you. It will seem, perhaps, that you do not even *want* to stop the sin, but that is a lie. Your new self earnestly desires for you to cease sinning and you know what God wants you to do. You do not need to listen to your feelings; listen to God's word. Cold-bloodedly, you must thrust the sin away, refusing to hear the pleas which your old nature will hurl at you:

"After all, you've been hurt! You're justified in feeling angry!"

"Your rights have been violated, you must defend them."

"Come on, this pleasure isn't really hurting anyone."

"If you behave sweetly, he'll think you're admitting that he's right! You can't do that! Where's your pride?"

Within you, also, is the voice of God's Spirit, firmly saying "No, God doesn't do things that way. Stop it." The Spirit will not push and shove and strive for your attention and that is why you are so easily distracted by the voices of sin. You must begin to get your hearing adjusted to that still, small voice or you will flounder.

Part of your problem is that you fail to realize the need to get free from the wrong reaction before you can manifest the right one. You cannot have on the old man and the new man at the same time. It does no good at all to sit there in the midst of a temper tantrum and ask God to take it away and fill you with love. The Spirit will not yank away your freely chosen sin-response. That is your job. It will not cease until you let it go. You must, by a heroic effort of your Christian will, die to your old sinful self, and reach instead for God's righteousness. As *you* let go of your bitterness, jealousy, criticism, lust and turn humbly to God, the *Spirit* will give you the love, patience, and self-control that you lack.

The hard part, of course, is the "letting go." Sometimes you must sin, and sin, and sin again, over and over like a broken record, before you are so sick of it that you want to let it go more than you want to hang onto it. Ask God to make you truly willing to stop, and he will. "God is always at work in you to make you *willing* and *able* to obey his own purpose" (Philippians 2:13).

God's word says: "We have died to sin—how, then, can we go on living in it? Our old being has been put to death with Christ on his cross, in order that the power of the sinful self be destroyed, so that we should no longer be slaves to sin" (Romans 6:1-11). Do you believe that? Your old self has been sentenced to death and was buried in a grave in Palestine almost 2,000 years ago, therefore, it has no business whatever affecting your life. God sees it as dead; you must force it to behave that way by burying it every time it rears its ugly head. It will mean saying to your old self a hundred times a day if necessary; "Stop it! I deny you the right to dominate me. You are dead, powerless, and I do not have to obey you. I refuse to do so right now." If you persist, it will begin to believe you mean it. The old self will not behave as if it were dead until it is convinced that you will tolerate no other behavior from it. That is a lifetime task.

Why is this never-ending battle against sin so important? Because, if you let it, the sin in you will destroy the life of God in you just as sin in the hearts of men destroyed the life of Christ on a Roman cross. Of all the hurt we have known, none is more tragic than the hurt of seeing a young Christian yield to sin over and over again until, finally, he is so hardened by it that he no longer desires to be free of it; or, if he does want to return to God, he finds that this is not easy because there has come a great buildup of resistance to God as a result of continual sin. Learn to walk so carefully that you can see temptations before you are in the midst of them. Thus, you will be steeled against their enticements.

As serious as is the dominion of sin, the dominion of despair after you have sinned is perhaps worse. It would be nice to think that all your misery over sin is caused by your love for righteousness, but that is not the case. Oswald Chambers has said "discouragement is disenchanted self-love."[2] Our egos are incredibly inflated, and we are appalled when we discover that we really cannot live as minisaints overnight. Sin should cause you to become more humble, repentant, contrite of heart, never angry and impatient with yourselves or with God. You are to be wrapped up in pleasing Jesus Christ, not in satisfying your egos with your own purity. God wants men and women who are so aware of their own spiritual poverty that they cast themselves happily upon God's mercy every time they sin, concentrating on the mercy, not the sin that made them seek it.

That is the proper reaction to sin: not discouragement, not anger, but joy! Not joy that you have sinned, but joy that it is forgiven the moment you admit it humbly and trust God for forgiveness. "If [you] confess [your] sins, he is faithful and just to forgive [your] sins, and cleanse [you] from all unrighteousness" (I John 1:9). That is a promise. If you believe it, you will not permit a moment of discouragement or fretting. God promises not only to forgive but also to cleanse. You must trust that he is at work in you to eradicate the sinful tendencies completely. Your inner joy can remain practically unaffected by sin if you deal with sin promptly and scripturally.

Belief in God's forgiveness includes belief in his forgetfulness. "I am he who blots out your transgressions . . . and I will not remember your sins" (Isaiah 43:25). If God has forgotten them, what business do you have remembering them!

You see, Jesus' whole purpose in coming was "that your joy may be full" (John 15:11). For that to happen, he had to die for your sins, so you should never have to fear that they might keep you from God. If you lose your joy because of sin, you are denying the gospel; you are saying that sin has great power and can affect your relationship with God. The Bible says "No, sin can no longer separate you from God, because Jesus has borne your guilt and punishment for you." So, act like a believer! Every time you sin you are putting your commitment and your faith to the test. Will you stop the sin? Will you let God's Spirit take over as you promised he could when you gave your life to Christ? Will you trust God for forgiveness? Will you choose joy over despair? Luther said, "sin boldly, but trust in Christ more boldly still." Trust in Christ can *always* cancel sin. You must fight sin with faith. If your faith is strong enough to enable you to remain joyful in spite of your sins and failures, you are indeed free from its dominion.

What will be the outcome of your persistent battle against sin? You will reap the fruit of righteousness. Jesus himself is "the author and finisher of our faith" (Hebrews 12:2 KJV). If we remain true to him he will see to it that we are "finished" properly! In Christ you get a glimpse of the unbelievable power and glory that can be unleashed in the human creature when every area of rebellion has been overthrown and the old nature is allowed no dominion. Jesus is the original grain of wheat and we are part of the harvest. We are ordained to resemble him because it is his life within us that is struggling so earnestly to manifest itself. Our Lord is faithful and will "present the church to himself, in all its beauty, pure and faultless, without spot or wrinkle or any other imperfection" (Ephesians 5:27). Praise God! As part of his church that is a promise for each of us—sinners now, but one day to be as perfect as the firstborn Son, free forever from the dominion of all but God himself.

NOTES

[1] Smith, Hannah Whitehall, *The Christian's Secret of a Happy Life*. Old Tappan, New Jersey, 1968.

[2] Chambers, Oswald, *My Utmost for His Highest*. New York: Dodd, Mead & Co., 1935, page 231.

13 Can I Believe What I Read in the Bible?

I'VE BEEN asked several thousand times, "Do you take the Bible literally? My answer is always the same: "I take the literal parts literally."

The Bible is a book containing many different kinds of writing: history, allegory, parable, prophecy, biography, metaphor, symbol, allusion. When Isaiah says, "the trees clap their hands" (Isaiah 55:12) I don't take it literally. I don't think Isaiah meant me to. When Jesus, in order to answer the question "who is my neighbor?" (Luke 10:23) tells the story of the Good Samaritan, I understand him to be doing just that—telling a story in order to answer a question. When John says the streets of heaven are paved with gold (Revelation 21:21), I realize that he is using physical imagery to describe a spiritual reality, and I don't get hung up on whether the gold is 14 or 21 carat.

The question of the literalness of Scripture is really two questions: Which parts are we *intended* to take literally and what are the grounds for doing so?

Sometimes, the first question is harder to answer than the second. When we read the story of Jonah, for example, and realize that the point of the story is not that he was swallowed by a fish, but rather that a group of Gentiles should be included in the mercy of the Jewish God, it may be hard to decide whether this is a miracle story or a parable. If it *is* a miracle story I have no problem accepting it. I believe in a God who performs miracles. He could easily have "appointed a great fish to swallow up Jonah" (Jonah 1:17) if he chose to do so. "Our God is in the heavens; he does whatever he pleases" (Psalm 115:3). Actually, we know that the sperm whale often swallows its young during violent storms and spits it out later safe and sound. Also, there have been instances reported of men living through just such an experience. Therefore, *if* the story of Jonah includes a miracle, it's not really a very big miracle, and, as we said, it's not the main point, anyway.

Most of the attacks on the authority of Scripture, however, arise from disbelief in the possibility that miracles really occur. Even leading theologians have said in essence, "we cannot take the story of the resurrection literally because literal resurrections do not happen." This is, of course, a circular argument, based not upon evidence, but upon an antisupernatural presupposition.

I don't honestly know whether the author of Jonah meant me to take the fish story literally, however, *I have no question whatsoever* that the authors of the New Testament meant me to take the resurrection story literally. Listen to Peter (II Peter 1: 16-18):

We have not depended on made-up legends in making known to you the mighty coming of our Lord Jesus Christ. With our own eyes we saw his greatness! We were there when he was given honor and glory by God the Father, when the voice came to him from the Supreme Glory, saying, "This is my own dear Son, with whom I am well pleased!" We ourselves heard this voice coming from heaven, when we were with him on the sacred mountain.

Similarly, John begins his first letter by specifying that he, too, was an eyewitness—not to a vision, but to real flesh-and-blood events that could be touched as well as seen (I John 1:1-4). Paul, after listing all of the various appearances of the risen Jesus, declares, "if Christ has not been raised from death ... we are shown to be lying against God, because we said of him that he raised Christ from death" (I Corinthians 15:14-15).

Let's not confuse things by calling the resurrection story a "parable" or a "myth." Very explicitly it claims to be literal fact. If it is not what it claims to be, the only alternative is that, as Paul wrote, it is a "lie against God."

Therefore, if the resurrection *is* true, I have very little difficulty with the lesser miracle stories throughout the Bible. If God could raise Jesus from the dead he could turn water into wine, or feed 5,000 people with a few loaves and fishes. While the question of miracles is important, the reliability of the Scriptures in general is really a much larger matter. That is, what are the grounds for accepting the Scriptures as authoritative? There seem to be three major criteria for doing so.

The first is *the increasing agreement of archaeological and historical investigation*. William F. Albright, late professor at the Johns Hopkins University, has stated unequivocally, "There can be no doubt that archaeology has confirmed the substantial historicity of the Old Testament tradition."[1] Nelson Glueck, reputed Jewish archaeologist, goes even further: "No archaeological discovery has ever controverted a Biblical reference."[2] (This is not, of course, to say that archaeology has proven all Biblical references to be true. It is startling, nevertheless, to admit that it has proven none, false!) Professor R. D. Wilson of Princeton put it this way,[3]

Nor, in spite of some apparent inconsistencies and of many passages difficult to explain satisfactorily, owing to an ignorance of all the facts, is there anything in the Old Testament that makes it appear incredible or unveracious. No one knows enough to affirm with confidence that any one of the prophetic books was not written by the man whose name it bears. No one knows enough to assert that the kings and others mentioned did not do and say what is ascribed to them.

Turning to the New Testament, Professor Frederick F. Bruce of the University of Manchester comments, "The evidence for our New Testament writings is ever so much greater than the evidence for many writings of classical authors, the authenticity of which no one dreams of questioning."[4] Bruce cites some of this evidence at far greater length than we can recount here, then concludes by quoting Sir Frederick Kenyon of the British Museum:[5]

The interval then between the dates of original composition and the earliest extant evidence becomes so small as to be in fact negligible, and the last foundation for any doubt that the scriptures have come down to us substantially as they were written has now been removed. Both the *authenticity* and the *general integrity* of the books of the New Testament may be regarded as finally established.

The Biblical story, Old and New Testaments, is, in all essentials, trustworthy. Wherever it has been checked by archaeology and/or secular history it has been verified repeatedly. In particular, the Gospel of Luke stands as a masterpiece of historical accuracy. It was Luke's expressed purpose to "write an orderly account for you . . . that you will know the full truth of all those matters which you have been taught" (Luke 1:3-4). Sir William Ramsey, beginning his career as an archaeologist quite skeptical of Luke's reliability, was finally compelled to conclude:[6]

Luke is a historian of the first rank; not merely are his statements of fact trustworthy; he is possessed of the true historic sense; he fixes his mind on the idea and plan that rules the evolution of history, and proportions the scale of his treatment to the importance of each incident. He seizes the important and critical events and shows their true nature at greater length, while he touches lightly or omits entirely much that was valueless for his purpose. In short, this author should be placed along with the very greatest of historians.

Luke's attention to detail is phenomenal. He roots events in externally verifiable history. He specifies names, dates, and places, and demonstrates extraordinary care in the use of the titles belonging to the various political persons involved. The other Gospels (which have slightly different purposes— John, for instance is more of a personal memoir) may be fitted into the historical outline given by Luke. All together they provide us with a picture of Jesus that is questionable only if we begin with the most hypercritical of presuppositions.

This, then, is the first criterion: The Biblical record is accurate historically. Archaeology has confirmed and reconfirmed its story, even to the extent that current expeditions are attempting to unearth, on the top of Mt. Ararat, a boat which many believe to be Noah's ark. In the center of the story, some of the most careful reporting the world has ever known concerns a man named Jesus.

The second criterion for confidence in the Scriptures concerns *Jesus himself*. Nowhere, do we find any of the Gospel writers claiming to write *every word* exactly as Jesus originally spoke it. Of course there is paraphrase and summary! All history textbooks condense and organize material; the New Testament authors did that, too. However, they claimed that their portrait of Jesus was *accurate in all essentials* concerning the things he said and did. As we turn to that portrait to discover what he taught regarding the authority of Scripture, we are struck by three inter-related statements:

1) The Old Testament is not just an accurate history book, it is *God's Word*;

2) Jesus taught that *his own words* were spoken only on authority from God; and

3) he said that when the time came for the apostles to write down his biography *they* would be aided by the Holy Spirit.

Let's examine these claims more fully.

First, Jesus saw "the Scriptures" (our Old Testament) as having come from God. Regarding the Law he said, "As long as heaven and earth last, the least point or the smallest detail of the Law will not be done away with" (Matthew 5:18). When tempted in the wilderness, his response was simply, "It is written!" (Matthew 4:4, 7, 10)—that being sufficient, in his opinion, to end all argument. With sweeping finality he declared, "what the Scripture says is true forever" (John 10:35).

Repeatedly, Jesus spoke of himself and the events surrounding his life as being the fulfillment of Biblical prophecies, most notably, perhaps, with regard to his crucifixion: "how slow you are to believe everything the prophets said! Was it not necessary for the Messiah to suffer these things and enter his glory? And Jesus explained to them what was said about him in *all* the Scriptures, beginning with the books of Moses and the writings of *all* the prophets" (Luke 24:25-26).

Jesus' regard for the Old Testament writings was so great that he frequently quoted passages as if they were the words of God himself. The New Testament writers followed him so closely in this that they reversed the identification on occasion. For example, Paul quotes Exodus 9:16 by saying *"the Scripture* says to Pharaoh, 'I made you king' " (Romans 9:17). This habitual identification of the words of Scripture with the words of God led him to the classic summation of the apostolic view: "All Scripture is inspired by God and is useful for teaching the truth, rebuking error, correcting faults, and giving instruction for right living, so that the man who serves God may be fully qualified and equipped to do every kind of good work" (II Timothy 3:16-17).

Second: Jesus claimed repeatedly that his own words were also the words of God himself. "What I teach is not mine, but comes from God, who sent me" (John 7:16). Directly and indirectly, by explicit statement and by moral example, by signs and wonders, by fulfilled prophecy and the resurrection from the dead, Jesus claimed to be God in the flesh—the promised Messiah—at the very least, one whose words could be trusted as absolute truth. To know him was to know God (John 8:19); to see him was to see God (John 12:45); to believe in him was to believe in God (John 12:44); to receive him was to receive God

(Mark 9:37); to hate him was to hate God (John 15:23); to honor him was to honor God (John 5:23).

In short, Jesus' claims regarding his own authority and his teaching regarding the Scriptures' authority go hand in hand. The two were really one. Thus, whenever Peter and the others preached about him their first words were always "this is what the prophets said," and they followed them immediately with "this is what Jesus did." They were one and the same.

Thirdly, Jesus went further. He promised this regarding the New Testament (John 14:25-26):

I have told you this while I am still with you. The Helper, the Holy Spirit whom the Father will send in my name, will teach you everything, and make you remember all that I have told you.

And again (John 15:26-27),

The Helper will come—the Spirit of truth, who comes from the Father. I will send him from the Father, and he will speak about me. And you, too, will speak about me, for you have been with me from the very beginning.

And yet again (John 16:12-15),

I have much more to tell you, but now it is too much for you to understand. But when the Spirit of truth comes, he will lead you into all the truth. He will not speak on his own, but he will tell you what he hears, and will speak of things to come. He will give me glory, for he will take what I have to say and tell it to you. All that my Father has is mine; that is why I said that the Spirit will take what I give him and tell it to you.

In short, Jesus is saying that while the New Testament can be an accurate historical account because its authors had eyewitness authority, it can be trusted a great deal more than that. Their accounts would be *recalled, interpreted,* and *supplemented by the Holy Spirit of God!*

This, then, is the second criterion regarding the reliability of the Scriptures: Both Old and New Testaments come to us with the stamp of Jesus' own authority. If you are committed to him, you are committed to his viewpoint. Note that this is not simply another circular argument ("Jesus' authority comes from the Bible, and the Bible's authority comes from Jesus"). It is, rather, the recognition that if the Bible is acceptable as history it must be a great deal more than just history.

It was this confidence—that their teaching was Spirit-inspired—that gave the apostles their exuberant authority. It was this that enabled Paul to write "If anyone supposes he is God's messenger or has a spiritual gift, he must realize that what I am writing you is the Lord's command" (I Corinthians 14:37). Note the way he distinguished between that teaching that he *knew* to be from the Lord, and that which was only his own considered opinion (I Corinthians 7:10, 25). Peter equated Paul's letters with "the other scriptures" (II Peter 3:16) thereby indicating that the leaders of the early Church considered them to have the same authority as did the Old Testament. The list of instances in which the apostles conspicuously claimed for their writing the authority Jesus promised could be extended almost indefinitely. The decisions of the Great Councils of the Early Church as to which books should be included in the New Testament were made on this basis: Which books had the two-fold stamp of authority, that of an eyewitness aided by the Holy Spirit of God?

All of the preceding brings us to the third and final criterion of the Bible's reliability: *The test of practical experience.* In the final analysis, the question of the authority of Scripture is not an academic issue at all but an immensely practical one. The Bible has often been called a "self-validating" book; that is, a book whose truth becomes evident as you dare to believe and act upon it. The Old Testament closes with a promise, indeed, a challenge: "Bring the full tithes into the storehouse . . . and thereby put me to the test, says the Lord of hosts, if I will not open the windows of heaven for you and pour down for you an overflowing blessing" (Malachi 3:10 RSV). The closing words of the New Testament contain a warning: "If anyone takes away anything from the prophetic words of this book, God will take away from him his share of the fruit of the tree of life" (Revelation 22:19). In short, belief and obedience lead to blessing; disbelief and disobedience destroy it. "Put me to the test," "claim my promises by faith," "seek me while I may be found," over and over the Scriptural challenge is to get in on the action. The Bible's reliability points inevitably to the fact that you should rely on it! It is verified for the believer by the agreement of history, the authority of Jesus, and the adventure of faith.

NOTES

1 Albright, William F., *Archaeology and the Religion of Israel*. Baltimore: Johns Hopkins Press, 1942, page 176.
2 Glueck, Nelson, *Rivers In the Desert*. New York: Farrar, Strauss and Giroux, Inc., 1959, page 31.
3 Quoted in Douglas Johnson, *The Christian and His Bible*. London: Inter-Varsity Fellowship, 1962, page 106, 107.
4 Bruce, Frederick F., editor, *The New Testament Documents: Are They Reliable?* Grand Rapids, Mich.: Wm. B. Eerdmans Publishing Co., 1959, page 15.
5 Quoted in Bruce, *ibid.*, page 20.
6 Quoted in Bruce, *ibid.*, page 91.

14 The Trinity

AT THE very center of Christianity stands a doctrine that nobody understands: the doctrine of the Trinity, the assertion that God is both Three and One at the same time. The more you try to understand it the more questions you seem to run into. Is the Holy Spirit really a separate person, or is this just a way of talking about Jesus living inside of you? If Jesus can be inside of you, how can he be "at the right hand of the Father?" For that matter, how can he be both God and man? As one girl put it, "the more I try to think about these things, the more I end up with a mental picture of three gods."

Well she might! The only way you can think of something you haven't directly experienced, is by comparing it with something you have directly experienced. Nobody has ever *experienced* the Trinity, and since it's quite unlike anything you have experienced, no really adequate analogy is possible. Yet, it's terribly important because either Jesus *is* God, or he *isn't;* either God *is* trinitarian, or he *isn't*. Perhaps several analogies taken together, each illustrating a slightly different point, will be helpful to us.

Let's think first of something rather like the idea of three gods. Suppose for a moment that you're a being from another world. You have come upon some literature from the planet Earth, and you have read a good deal about that strange creature called "Man." You've read, for instance, what Aristotle said about him, that he is a "rational animal." You have decided to visit Earth, to meet this "Man" for yourself. Upon your arrival you encounter the Joneses: Daddy Jones, Mommie Jones, and little Baby Jones. You ask them, "Where is Man?"

Of course, they can't show you "Man"—they can only show you individual *men*, themselves. *"Man is a collective reality*. Somehow that one single "Man" that Aristotle referred to is composed of three Joneses, along with about three billion other human beings who populate the earth. To realize this, and to say that "Man" cannot be found apart from individual "men," is not to say that "Man" is *unreal*. Rather, it is to say that his reality is *more complex* than the reality of individual entities. "Man" *is* three billion men!

In a somewhat similar way, Christianity says that God *is* three "Persons." There's a difference, however, which we'll try to explain in a moment, but, first, let's consider another common example.

One of the ancient creeds says that Jesus is "of one substance with the Father." But what is a "substance?" The dictionary says it is "that which underlies all outward manifestations: the real, unchanging essence or nature of a thing." The example, of course, is water. Water remains water even though it may be found in a liquid, a gaseous, or a solid state. The real "substance" of water remains unchanged beneath all of its outward manifestations, just as the real "substance" of "human nature" remains unchanged beneath the outward manifestations of three billion individual personalities. So, the "substance" of God remains unchanged, though it is to be found in the "manifestations" of Father, Son, and Holy Spirit.

The difficulty with both of these first two analogies is that, while we may speak of "individual manifestations," no single manifestation is necessary to the definition of the "substance" of either "Man" or "water." If the world were the sort of place where water never froze, water would still be water even though it could then be found only as liquid or gas. Similarly, if a single human personality were removed from the world's population, the definition of "human nature" would remain unchanged. However, when it is said that "God is three Persons" it means that to remove any one of them would be to change the nature of God altogether. So you must look for yet another example and perhaps the readiest will be found in geometry.

Consider a triangle, for example. It is three sides. Each side has a separate, individual reality of its own; take any one side away from the triangle and you don't have a triangle any longer. Take one side away from a square, and you don't have a square any longer. Take one square away from a cube, and you don't have a cube any longer. C. S. Lewis used this example when he wrote[1]

On the human level one person is one being, and any two persons are two separate beings—just as, in two dimensions (say on a flat sheet of paper) one square is one figure, and any two squares are two separate figures. On the Divine level you still find personalities; but up there you find them combined in new ways which we, who do not live on that level, cannot imagine. In God's dimension, so to speak, you find a being who is three Persons while remaining one Being, just as a cube is six squares while remaining one cube.

Lewis goes on to suggest that if we lived in a world of only two dimensions we could never properly imagine figures like cubes, but only squares and triangles. If we lived in a world of only one dimension, we could never imagine squares and triangles, but only straight lines. And, in a world of no dimensions, we could imagine no lines at all, but only individual points.

Therefore, we cannot properly imagine the complexity of God, precisely because his "world" *is* more complex than ours. Or, more accurately, because ours—our whole world— is only a small part of his.

Do you see now what is wrong with thinking of three gods? You may speak of three men, each of whom is "a man," but you may not properly speak of the three Persons who are God as three separate gods. While Father, Son, and Holy Spirit are in some ways like three men (for example, the three Joneses), they are in other ways like the three sides of a triangle, inextricably bound together.

There is yet another analogy, the one Jesus used most frequently himself. While the sides of a triangle or a square have no particular relationship to each other (except that of being adjacent), the members of a *family* do have particular relationships to each other. All the Joneses are Joneses, but Daddy Jones is not Mommy Jones, Mommy Jones is not Baby Jones, and Baby Jones is not Daddy Jones. So, Jesus said, on the one hand, "I and my Father are one" (John 10:30 RSV)—in the sense that both are God—and, on the other, he said, "My Father is greater than I" (John 14:28 RSV) denoting thereby a relationship within God himself. The Father is not the Son, and the Son is not the Father, yet both are God. Such a relationship is not static like that between the sides of a triangle. It is alive and personal, pulsating and vital, like the relationships between members of a human family. The analogy may be pressed a bit further yet.

Even within a human family, the relationships between the members of the family may become so alive, so vital, that you speak of a "family spirit." You may notice that the members of the family actually behave and speak differently when they are together than when they are apart from each other. It is almost as if the "family spirit" becomes a kind of shared personality, a thing in itself, at such times. In a somewhat similar fashion, again, the relationship Jesus has with his Father is so real, is so alive, that it is a separate Personality within God. The "family spirit" between the Father and Son is what Jesus referred to as the Holy Spirit.

It is important to remember at this point that the family relationships within God did not begin with the incarnation of Jesus. They have been going on from eternity. God has *always* been Father, Son, and Holy Spirit; he has always been more excitingly and complexly real than anything you and I can imagine. Thus, the "Spirit of God" appears repeatedly throughout the Old Testament, and there are occasional intriguing instances of dialogue within the Being of God such as that at the very outset of the Book of Genesis when God says "let *us* make man in *our* image." When God appears to men in the Old Testament, it is invariably as "one like the Son of God" who walked among Shadrach, Mesach, and Abednego in the fiery furnace.

The staggering wonder of Christianity is not that the God who was One should suddenly become Three. The wonder is that the God who has always been Father, Son, and Holy Spirit should so humble himself as to become a man in the Person of the Son; that God, who has been God from all eternity, should love us enough to become a little baby in the stinking squalor of a stable; that the mighty God who created heaven and earth should endure spitting and scourging, ridicule and rejection; that God should be nailed in naked contempt on a cross of crucifixion, with angry flies buzzing about his untended wounds—to save those who put him there from their own folly and destruction!

That's the doctrine of the Trinity: not something that should bend your mind, but something that should break your heart. It arose not as a matter of philosophy, but as a matter of history. Two thousand years ago there appeared on the shores of the Mediterranean, in a little village in Palestine, a human being who was obviously a man, yet undeniably more than one. He ate, he slept, he got tired, he cried, he was born of a human mother yet he claimed to share God's nature in a way that other men could not dismiss as lunacy or a demonic lie. They recognized in him the God they had known through the prophets and kings and they marvelled as he exercised the power and prerogatives of God while remaining a man. They heard him predict that he would die and rise again—and they watched it happen. They heard him promise to send his Spirit to live within their hearts so that they, even they, could share with him that relationship with the Father that was his alone. They came to know that Spirit of God within them in a way that not a single one of them ever understood fully enough to explain adequately. Yet, this Spirit has transformed the lives of generation upon generation of those who believed and through them, it has changed the world.

Of course, it is the Spirit of God, and not Christ himself, who lives within men's hearts. The confusion is understandable. The New Testament writers, themselves, often called the Holy Spirit "the Spirit of Jesus," and, as we saw in the last chapter, it is the function of the Spirit to point to Christ. "He shall take what is mine and declare it to you" (John 16:15 RSV). Thus, when you say "I asked Jesus to come into my life," you are really using a kind of shorthand for saying "I asked Jesus' Spirit—the Spirit of the living God—to come into my life."

God became a man to reveal the unimaginable. It was his purpose to rescue you from the consequences of your sin, so he himself bore its pain. It was his purpose to unite you with himself, so he united himself with you—in the Person of the Son. The Trinity remains unimaginable and, for most people, the attempt to picture it really produces not with "three gods," but with three men, three human beings. You picture God as you picture Jesus—and this is just as God intended. He became a man so you *could* imagine a little bit of what he's like. The Christian is one who bets his life that God will turn out to be like Jesus.

Don't be worried, therefore, if your mental picture of the Trinity is that of three Men, each of whom resembles a Galilean carpenter. Remember, the picture is not the reality itself. "No man has ever seen God; the only Son, who is in the bosom of the Father, he has made him known" (John 1:18 RSV).

NOTES

1 Lewis, C. S., *Mere Christianity*. New York: The Macmillan Company, 1960, page 126.

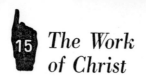
15 The Work of Christ

JUST AS you are born into a human family without understanding the "facts of life," so it is possible to be born
into God's family without fully understanding the facts of
new life. It is important, however, that you try to do so,
both for your own sake and for the sake of others.

You know, of course, that Christ died for your sins, and
that somehow God's forgiveness of them hinges on that fact
of history. How does it? What is the relationship between
the death of Jesus on a Roman cross 2,000 years ago and
your standing before Almighty God today?

We have waited until now to deal with this question—
which is really the central question of the Christian faith—
because an adequate answer depends upon your having
some understanding of what was covered in the last chapter.
*How the death of Jesus, 2,000 years ago, affects you today
depends entirely upon who Jesus really was.* The Christian
claim is that he was born "truly God," and "truly man," and
that his death must, therefore, be understood in *both* of
those aspects.

Perhaps it is easier to understand the human aspect first
because his becoming a man was done that we might understand him in human terms. As a human being, Jesus stepped
into your shoes, and mine, and received the punishment
that should have been ours. At the very outset of all human
history God told Adam that sin must lead to death (Genesis 2:17).

If you understand this only in terms of physical death
you will miss the point entirely. Death was (is) essentially
separation from God, a broken relationship, discord where
before there had been harmony. Turning your back upon
God, ignoring him and trying to live independently is sin.
If God is the Author of Life, then turning your back on him

must inevitably mean embracing Life's only alternative. Every form of discord throughout society, and in the hearts of individual men, is a working out of this fundamental discord between men and God. "Death" is at work wherever there is sin. Physical death is but a more obvious manifestation of this deeper, more profound, spiritual condition Notice that the prophets in the Old Testament do not say, "Because of your sins you *will die*." Instead, they announce, "You *are dead* in sins and trespasses." They say so over and over and over.

This might be understood *biologically* as the result of having poisoned yourself by sinning. It might be understood *legally* as the punishment to which you have been sentenced for your crimes. In either case, as your fellow human being, Jesus steps into your place and accepts the terrible consequences of what you have done—*in order to save you from them*. He can only do this if he is fundamentally different from the rest of mankind regarding the "sickness" or the "crime." He can offer you a heart transplant only if his own is not defective. When the penalty was death, he could pay it for you only if he, himself, did not deserve to die. This, of course, is exactly what the New Testament proclaims about him. He was "tempted in every way that we are, but did not sin" (Hebrews 4:15).

One of the central features of Old Testament religion was the sacrificing of animals as "scapegoats" in the place of those who had broken God's Law (everyone) and deserved to die. Sin was symbolically transferred from the people to an innocent animal, usually a goat, which was then driven off into the wilderness to die. Sheep, cattle, doves, and pigeons were also sacrificed to *atone* (set "at-one") for sin.

In the New Testament Jesus is repeatedly called a Lamb "who takes away the sin of the world" (John 1:29). His death is seen as having done perfectly, once and for all, what the Old Testament sacrifices did incompletely and in a limited way (Hebrews 10:11-12). It was not merely the replacing of one "system" with another, however. From the Biblical perspective, the death of Christ was *always* the pivotal point in man's relationship with God. The Old Testament sacrifices never stood alone, or accomplished anything in and of themselves, according to Christian belief. They anticipated, or "foreshadowed," the death of Jesus. "a faint outline of the good things to come" (Hebrews 10:1). Much in the way that a man's shadow precedes him into a room, if the sun is at his back, giving a hint of what he looks like, so the Jewish sacrifices came first chronologically, but the real atoning came with the sacrifice of Jesus.

Some years ago, the head counselor of a boys' summer camp was faced with a difficult problem. One of the campers had misbehaved so consistently and seriously as to make life miserable for staff and campers. He came from a bad home situation, and sending him back would not only have made things worse for him but it would have seemed like an admission of failure on the part of the camp. The boy had lied, stolen, committed petty vandalism, tormented younger campers, and so on and on. What should be done? Finally, the counselor called all of his staff together and brought the boy before them. "You deserve to be whipped," he said quietly. And then a moment later he added, "but I will take it for you." And, that is what he did. As the boy watched with terrified eyes and quivering lips, he removed his shirt and *took* the blows as one of the other counselors carried out the whipping the boy deserved. Suddenly, the boy began to cry. For a long time, he sobbed quite uncontrollably. When at last he stopped he was a different person. Whereas the whipping might have been too much for him to take, or might have made him even more hostile, had he received it himself, seeing someone who was innocent take it for him broke his heart.

So it is with Jesus. As an innocent Man he puts himself

in the place of sinful men, accepts their punishment, and it breaks their hearts.

However, Jesus was also God. Remembering this makes the mystery of his death even more profound. People have often said, "I can appreciate the compassion of Jesus in dying for us, but how could God require it of him? How is it righteous to punish an innocent man on behalf of a guilty one? If sin needed to be punished, then it needed to be punished, and Jesus' death did not punish it. If, on the other hand, God wanted to forgive us, why didn't he simply do it? What was the need for a sacrifice at all?"

Let's go back to the head counselor and the boy. From one point of view the counselor was allowing an innocent person to suffer on behalf of a guilty one, true enough. From another point of view, he was demonstrating the fact that *in disregarding the counselor's rules the boy was hurting others*: other campers, other staff members, and the head counselor himself who had issued the rules in the first place. He was saying to the boy, "I forgive you, but I want you to know that it costs me something to do it." Notice carefully that it was the rule-breaking itself that hurt; the punishment was necessary so that the boy would realize it.

When I was fourteen, my uncle allowed me to drive his car before I had the training, or a license to drive. I smashed it up. He forgave me, but forgiveness meant that *he had to pay for having it repaired*. Another time I ruined a friend's sport coat. He, too, forgave me, but the forgiveness itself did not restore the coat miraculously. *He had to pay for it.*

The same thing is true in less material ways. Whenever you hurt another person with an unkind word or a thoughtless action that other person may react in one of two ways. He may become angry and try to "pay you back" for what you have done, or he may forgive you and accept the hurt without retaliation. But "accepting the hurt" means *it hurts!*

If he chooses not to "pay you back" in a very real sense he is "paying for it himself." Forgiveness *means* allowing you to hurt him, and loving you anyway.

When men rejected God, turned from him and ignored his teaching, despised his laws, killed his prophets, abused each other, ruined his world, worshiped idols, and became perverted and corrupt in every imaginable way—*it hurt him*! When he came among men in the physical human form of a man, and that same rejection was carried out to its logical extreme, attempting to destroy him altogether, *it hurt.*

Forgiveness means he took the hurt. He embraced it in all of its fullness. He allowed it to hurt without retaliation. Without paying men back for all they did to him, God paid for it himself—in Jesus. "If God wanted to forgive men, why didn't he simply do it?" That is precisely what he did!

Do you see the point? If the death of an innocent Man on your behalf breaks your heart, how much more will the recognition of Who that Man really is do? "If the blood of bulls and of goats, and the ashes of an heifer sprinkling the unclean, sanctifies to the purifying of the flesh, how much more shall the blood of Christ, who through the eternal Spirit offered himself without spot to God, purge your conscience from dead works to serve the living God?" (Hebrews 9:13, 14 KJV).

That, in short, is the doctrine of the atonement and the work of Christ. An innocent Man who was more than a man set other men at one with himself by refusing to reject them when they rejected him. Or, in St. Paul's words, "God was in Christ, reconciling the world to himself, not counting their trespasses against them" (II Corinthians 5:19 RSV) Amen, and Praise Him.

What About All Those Who Haven't Heard of Christ?

TOBY WAS rooming with an international student from Taiwan, who was a Buddhist. He came in one day, with tears in his eyes. "I know that Christ is the answer for me, but what about my roommate? What about Mohammedans and Hindus? What about those who have never even heard about Christ? Is it fair for God to judge people for not believing in someone they never heard of? If he's that sort of God, how can we call him loving?"

If he's "that sort of God," we can't! But he isn't.

God doesn't ask men to believe in Jesus because he wanted to make a narrow little pathway to himself which would exclude most of the men who ever lived and enable only a very few to make it. God asks men to believe in Jesus because *Jesus is God, and God is Jesus*! God is asking men to believe in him—in the God-who-became-man, the only God there is—not in some nonexistent sort of god they dream up.

The question is whether or not the God of the "sincere" Buddhist, or the "earnest" Mohammedan is, also, the real God. If there is really only one God, you either worship him, or you do not, and if you worship something other than the true God, your worship is idolatry. It's as simple as that.

A great many people seem to feel that faith in itself is a noble thing, pleasing to God. Nonsense! It isn't just any faith which pleases God, it's faith *in God himself*! God wants you to trust him instead of the other things you trust. Why? Because he cannot help you unless you do. A drowning man must trust the lifeguard or he will not be saved. If he trusts in himself or in someone who is not able to save him he won't get back to shore alive. God *wants* to save *all* men, but it is necessary that they trust themselves to him before he can save them.

When Jesus said "I am the way, the truth, and the life, no man comes to the Father but by me," he wasn't being narrowminded by trying to make men drop their perfectly good religions and turn to him instead. He was saying it because he knew that other religions weren't adequately bringing men to God the Father. He was simplifying, clarifying, the truth about God that already existed in the world, and, in doing so, he was pointing up the foolishness and error that existed as well. By saying, "believe in me," Jesus was telling men to "believe in God," because there is no other God! To believe in any other god is to believe in a figment of human imagination, or an evil spirit. God wasn't making it harder to find him when he came to earth in Jesus; he was making it much simpler, enabling men to see just what he was like so they could stop worshiping false gods and turn to the true God.

If worshiping Jesus is really worshiping the one true God, then worshiping the one true God must be worshiping Jesus, mustn't it? A man who worships the true God, whether or not he has ever heard of Jesus, would find Jesus attractive and worthy of worship if, and when, he did hear about him. A man who knows God the Father will rejoice to discover God the Son and will recognize the family resemblance! The point, then, isn't in the name you give to God. The point is whether or not the God you worship, under any name, is the true God of heaven and earth. That God is just as Jesus revealed him to be. By Jesus we measure the earth's religions and evaluate the gods men worship.

Think of all the great men of faith in the Old Testament whom God accepted long before Christ ever walked the earth. They were trusting the God of justice and mercy who offered them forgiveness of sins if they repented and sought, in earnest, to obey him. They didn't know that one day the Son of God would come and die upon a cross for their redemption, and yet God forgave them. Why? Because, since, from God's point of view, Jesus is "the Lamb slain from before the foundation of the world," the death of Jesus for sinful men was effective long before it actually took place on a Roman cross. God is the sort of God who bears the pain and rejection of men; he is a God who loves righteousness and honors righteous, faithful men. If that is the sort of God you trust in, you are trusting in the true God and he will honor and accept your faith. And, if that is your kind of God, then, naturally, you will love Jesus when you finally hear about him, because that's the sort of Person Jesus is, too!

You see, God has forgiven men all along only because Christ died for them. He never, anywhere, demands, however, that all men understand that fact with crystal clarity. Christ's blood will be effective for anyone who loves God, loves righteousness, seeks forgiveness, and hopes in God's mercy. The thief on the cross next to Jesus undertood virtually nothing about the incredible cosmic drama going on next to him, and yet, he reached out in faith to One who seemed to be as God ought to be: righteous, patient, loving, forgiving. With mercy, Jesus, who is God, accepted the man's minimal faith and assured him that he would find salvation that very day. No doubt it astonished the man when he learned, after his death, that it was through the blood of Christ that his sins had been forgiven and paradise made his! As the Psalms promise over and over, he reached out to the Lord and the Lord delivered him, although he comprehended little of the means by which his deliverance was secured.

But what about the man who has never heard of Jesus? How can God expect him to hold an accurate understanding of God's true character?

Both the Old and New Testaments say that even the man

who has never heard a word about God (much less about Jesus) still has sufficient evidence of God's reality and character, given to him in Creation itself, to respond to God with real faith. Psalm 19 tells us that the skies, the stars and planets, the earth itself, all proclaim that God is powerful and glorious, worthy of praise and honor. Although the elements can't actually speak, "their voice has gone out throughout all the earth and their words to the end of the world" (Psalm 19:4). Paul wrote to the Roman Christians that men are "without excuse, because although they knew God [through natural wonders and through conscience] they did not honor him as God or give thanks to him" (Romans 1:20-21). God *has* given to *all* men some evidence of his character. If the most simple and uneducated man in the world recognizes that the universe is the handiwork of a being greater and mightier than he, if he honors, thanks, and worships this Creator, seeking to know him better and obey him, repenting of the evil he has done to his fellow men (who are part of this being's creation), God will accept that man. What joy and wonder will be his when he finally learns, perhaps not until the moment after his death, who that God is and what he has done through Christ. Peter said in Acts 10, "I now realize that it is true that God treats all men alike. Whoever fears him and does what is right is acceptable to him, no matter what race he belongs to." He spoke thus to a Gentile, a Roman soldier. After Peter told him all about Jesus, the man gladly accepted Christ and God's Spirit came upon him. Because he loved God, he loved Jesus when he heard about him.

This, of course, is not what usually happens. The primitive in the jungle, just as the cultured scholar in America, worships himself. He rejects the revelation of God, whether elementary or complete. He make idols of stone in the jungle, or idols of money in the bank, and in so doing he becomes futile in his thinking . . . claiming to be wise, he becomes a fool . . . exchanging the truth about God for a lie and worshiping and serving the creature rather than the Creator (Romans 1:19-23 RSV). And so, he is, as Paul said, "without excuse."

You must be rather careful when you attempt to apply this teaching to members of organized religions other than Christianity. For while the common notion is that "all religions are basically the same," they are, in fact, strikingly different from each other. While, in many cases, ethically they say the same thing, that is, they contain the golden rule in some form, they are not in any way the same when they speak of God. Buddha and Confucious, for instance, both remained agnostics—some would say atheists—all of their lives. Mohammed denied resoundingly that he was God, or a god, or a part of God. He deplored his own sinfulness, confessing on his deathbed that he knew that he was still as far from God as he had been at the outset of his ministry. Ghandi, the "noblest Hindu of all time," said much the same thing on his deathbed.

In fact, if you search the world's religions, you will find that, apart from a few very small cults which society has recognized as obviously lunatic from the outset, no major religious figure in the history of the world has ever claimed for himself the things Christ claimed for *himself*. You will find men of great moral excellence, in some cases. But those of greatest excellence seem, like Ghandi, to be most deeply conscious of their own shortcomings. Then, you will find the few who have made radical claims to divinity dismissed by the world as insane because they have no moral excellence at all. Indeed, it may be stated unequivocally that in Jesus Christ we have history's unique example of a man who *claimed* to be God and *acted* like it!

Thus, those who worship human beings, even great human beings, are on very dangerous ground. Even if they are sincere in their belief, their sincerity does not change the fact that they are in error, and, indeed, that their belief is in direct opposition to the facts. God does not honor "faith" in anything, or in anyone. The *object* of faith is the all-important factor. Those who worship persons or things have "exchanged the truth about God for a lie, and worshipped and served the *creature* rather than the Creator."

So, we must be careful. Is the "sincere" Buddhist sincere in following Buddha's teachings, which are primarily ethical, agreeing with those of Christ so far as they go, or is he sincere in elevating to a position of blasphemous and idolatrous worship a fellow human being who—for all his fine teaching—remained a sinful creature?

The Bible states very clearly that all men have some light and truth. The question is really whether or not they live up to the amount of real truth about God which they do possess. The primitive in the jungle who knows that God isn't a huge stone monster (which couldn't create anything, much less the world), who knows that, whatever God is, he does not approve of human sacrifice, yet acquiesces in those things because he is in superstitious bondage to the customs of his tribe, is not living up to the truth that he holds in his heart.

It is a spiritual fact that if we do live up to the light God gives us, he will give us more. If we never cry, "Stop! That's far enough, I will go no farther!" we will make continual spiritual progress. Amy Carmichael describes an Indian woman named Mimosa[1] who, at a very young age, visited a Christian missionary compound and for a few hours was exposed to some Christian teaching. She returned to her home, but was a changed girl. From that day on she refused to follow her family tradition of reverence for the god Shiva. She had another God now, a God of love. As she grew to womanhood and was married she shamed her family and husband with her continuing refusal to worship the family deities. She tried to raise her children with some knowledge of the true God about whom she herself knew practically nothing. During times of great poverty and sickness she would petition her God, and, faithfully, he provided for her needs. Risking persecution, rejection, starvation, she remained faithful to the Light she had, always praying that somehow, sometime, she might be permitted to return to the Christian community where she could learn more of the God she loved and served. Finally, God did lead Mimosa back to the missionary community where she was granted the joy of discovering Jesus and hearing the Gospel message which she readily accepted.

God will nourish and protect true faith, wherever it appears, no matter how small and ill-informed it may be, in the hope that it will come to flourish and blossom into a strong, knowledgeable trust in him. God alone, however, is the judge, both of the Light received and of the Light obeyed, and you must believe that he judges with infinite love, infinite justice, and does not err.

What about those, however, who *have* heard of Jesus and have refused to believe in him? What is it about Jesus that they reject? Can you see that it is contradiction for them to claim to believe in God, and yet refuse to accept his Son? The god they are clinging to is a god of their own imagination—not the God who has revealed himself in history. If they balk at accepting God as Jesus portrayed him, they will certainly balk at the thought of spending eternity with such a God! You may hear people say, "I believe that Jesus was a great prophet, but I cannot believe that he was literally God. I like his teachings, but I can't believe that he was more than just a very good man." It is easy to say that you like someone's teachings or to adhere to a certain philosophy. Those teachings, however, take on an entirely different character if it suddenly becomes clear that they are actually true, the teachings of the one true God, maker of heaven and earth. If that's the case, then they must be obeyed, taken with the utmost seriousness. As long as Jesus is "just a good man," his teachings can be picked over, accepted, or rejected according to the tastes of each individual. If he is God, there are only two choices: obedience or outright rebellion. Most people, not wanting to be faced with that fearful choice, refuse to consider Jesus as God's divine spokesman. The issue is not really intellectual trouble with the doctrine of the incarnation; it is unwillingness to submit to God's righteousness and to entrust God with your entire life.

And, God permits you to dodge the issue in this way, if you wish. He respects you too much to violate your personality and force you to serve him if you don't want to. But, if you don't want to serve him, you must accept the consequences of your free choice. Eternal separation from God is the inevitable result of choosing to separate yourself from him during this life.

What a responsibility Christians have, therefore, to help others grow from a vague, confused faith into true knowledge of Jesus Christ! Our question should not be, "what is the minimal sort of faith that God accepts?" but rather, "how can we best illuminate the minds and hearts of people so that they see, in Jesus, what God is really like and come to trust him?" As we make ourselves available to him, God will use us to bring others to the sort of faith he requires. And we must trust him all the way, believing that he is a God of love, and that he judges men according to their hearts, always judging fairly.

NOTES

[1] Carmichael, Amy, *Mimosa*. Fort Washington, Pa.: Christian Literature Crusade, 1958.

17 How Can a Good God Allow Suffering?

IN A philosophy class a student wrote, "When you see somebody dying of cancer, writhing with pain, it becomes pretty hard to go on talking about the love of God as if all were sweetness and light. In fact, it becomes pretty hard to talk about the love of God at all."

Of all the questions Christians face, this one is probably the most devastating. If God is good, why does he allow so much suffering to exist? If he really loves us, why does he permit sickness, mental disease, accidental tragedy, and man-caused evil to hurt us? Embittered people often conclude either that God cannot alleviate suffering, or that he just doesn't want to. In either case, they say, they will not worship a God so weak or so lacking in compassion. How does the Christian view all this?

Since the Christian believes that the character and intentions of God have been fully revealed in Jesus, he looks to the attitudes and actions of his Lord regarding this question, as he does regarding every other.

Jesus must have seen a great deal of sickness, poverty, and cruelty, because Palestine was not a wealthy place and the Roman legions weren't known for their gentleness to captive peoples. Then, too, many wondered, "Why?" as infants died from hunger and the aged lived out useless lives as crippled beggars, and the lepers lived as outcasts. For Jesus the answer was clear: God loves them all and wants them healed. Thus, his mission of revealing God's will involved primarily the administration of God's power in healing, forgiving, releasing men and women throughout Palestine from pain, poverty and sin. "The blind can see, the lame can walk, the lepers are made clean, the deaf hear, the dead are raised . . . and the Good News is preached to the poor" (Matthew 11:5).

Jesus commissioned his disciples to heal as well (Matthew 10:1), thereby assuring us that his own ministry was not merely a demonstration of God's power *in him* but that it is God's will, always, for all of his children to bind up wounds and strengthen the weak in spirit.

Why, then, are so many still suffering? Why do prayers for healing so often seem to go unanswered? Jesus knew the frustration of being unable to heal. In his home town there was so little faith in him that he—the Son of God— was unable to channel God's healing power to the sick and needy (Matthew 13:58). And, his disciples experienced defeat as well, due both to the nature of some diseases and their own weak faith (Mark 9:14-27). Is it really any wonder that in our own day, when skepticism runs rampant and even Christians are afraid to believe that God can heal bodies and minds, we see so little evidence of God's power?

God hasn't ceased caring for the suffering! It is still his will today, as it was in Jesus' time, for all men to be well and strong, whole in mind and body as well as in spirit. You and I are commanded to pray for the sick, and to expect God to hear and answer (James 5:14-16). We are taught that Christ bore our diseases as well as our sins (Isaiah 53:4), so that we need not submit any longer to their dominion. If we cannot believe that, if we fail to exercise the authority that we now have over such things, we mustn't blame God if the sick are not restored. God's will hasn't changed, but neither have his conditions. There are many miracles being done today by men and women who have discovered their roles as Christ's representatives and are daring, by faith, to cast out demons and lay hands on people, expecting them to recover.

"Where is the God of Elijah?" someone once asked. "He is waiting for an Elijah to call upon him!" was the answer. God hasn't stopped caring.

There is, however, another side to the coin. Suffering

and death, itself, are the consequences of sin; as such, they will remain a malignant part of the Creation until the end of the age. But God's purposes are not thwarted by this. The teaching is clear; "we know that in *all things* [pain and suffering included] God works for good with those who love him, those whom he has called according to his purpose" (Romans 8:28). Paul wrote, "we rejoice in our sufferings, knowing that suffering produces endurance, and endurance produces character, and character produces hope, and hope does not disappoint us, because God's love has been poured into our hearts through the Holy Spirit which has been given to us" (Romans 5:3-5 RSV).

Think of how this progression is exactly opposite to the usual experience of a sufferer. Suffering usually produces not patience, but impatience (with oneself, one's circumstances, one's family). Impatience, rather than building character, leads to its disintegration, with the sufferer becoming bitter, unhappy, finding fault with those around him. Finally, this degeneration of character leads not to hope, but to despair, and you hear from the lips of the sufferer—when the pain is great enough, or long enough—that most tragic of phrases, "I want to die!"

I watched my father wrestle with multiple sclerosis and go from one unhappy stage to the next in just this order. Then, I watched with joy and wonder as my father began to trust God's promises, and believe that, in spite of his disability, in the very midst of pain, God's love was real and for him. In a total reversal of the progression, Paul's words came true before my eyes! My father, who had not known Christ before his illness, is now preparing for the ministry in the midst of that illness!

Mrs. Wagner was in an old people's home, crippled, suffering from psoriasis, destitute, having lost her husband and only son twenty years before—absolutely radiant with joy! Her secret? "When everything else was taken from me

I discovered that God himself is sufficient for my every need."

Jesus prayed that the cup of suffering might pass from him (Matthew 26:39). But it didn't. God extended the incomparable benefits of salvation to us by denying this, his well-beloved Son's most urgent request in his neediest hour.

The implication should be clear. God never initiates your suffering, but he sometimes permits it. When he does so—whether by sickness, bereavement, accident, or persecution—you may be confident that he'll turn it to positive good, *if you let him*!

Pain and suffering are just as great opportunities (maybe greater) for blessing as any other experiences of life. As with any other experiences of life, however, they can be occasions for rebellion, disobedience, and turning from God. Ernest Gordon described in his amazing book, *Miracle on the River Kwai*, the utter demoralization that prevailed in the Japanese prison camps set up along the Kwai River during World War II. Thousands of Allied prisoners died from malnutrition, overwork, and disease. Tortures of a horrible variety were applied vindictively and savagely. Men gave up hope and began stealing from the dying and bribing guards for extra crumbs of rotten bread.

A miracle occurred, however, when a handful of Christians began to reverse this trend. These men gave away their meager portions of food to those more sick than they. They used their precious sleeping hours to tend the sick and dying. Here and there, men began to take hope and the Spirit of Christ caught hold of the imaginations of these hapless creatures. They found life and joy in serving others, in camps where there was no alternative source of happiness. Service and love were the only things that gave life meaning, the only things that kept them from total degeneration. A Bible Study began when one man managed to smuggle in some portions of scripture copied laboriously by hand. Sunday worship services were held as men's interest in God sprang into new life. Men were healed, lives were saved and transformed; a sense of purpose and excitement permeated the camp. There, in the midst of excruciating suffering, God's will was being done and the change was electric to all involved.

There were those, however, who refused to be caught up in such a revival of the human—and divine—spirit. There are always those who seem to prefer bitterness and recrimination to the joyful acceptance of suffering as an opportunity for love and growth. Suffering, turned to God, seems so often the supreme producer of sainthood. Jesus himself, says the writer to the Hebrews, "learned to be obedient by means of his sufferings" (Hebrews 5:8).

God has revealed to you and me that the end of things will be more wonderful than we can imagine. God's new heaven and new earth (see Chapter 19) will be filled with joyful men and women, and there will be no tears, no pain, no evil, no sin, no death (Revelation 21:4). This is God's will for men, and in his own time he will bring it to pass. Paul wrote that the suffering we undergo today *is not worth comparing* with the glory that will be ours when we are joined to Christ for eternity (Romans 8:18).

Until then, the suffering itself provides a necessary ingredient in the makeup of that glory.

God could have created a world without evil. He could have ordered the universe so that neither evil nor its consequences of pain and suffering were possible. However, had he done so, choice would have had no meaning. While you and I would have been kept from sinning, we also would be kept from righteousness—both come only by choice—and we would be no more "created in God's image, than would a mechanical robot.

Instead, God made a real world, with real choices and real consequences, some of which hurt, and some of which fall indiscriminately on all of us. Such a world prepares us for living—as real people, not as robots—in the more perfect world to come.

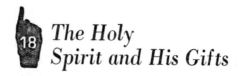

18 *The Holy Spirit and His Gifts*

THE AMAZING gift of God to his children is his own Holy Spirit. This Gift contains God's Life and Nature; it is this Gift, resident within us, that makes us God's children.

Does everyone possess the Holy Spirit?

Scripture gives you some definite clues to help you know whether or not you, or anyone, possess God's Holy Spirit. St. Paul, in his great discussion on the charismatic gifts of the Spirit, says that "no one can say 'Jesus is Lord!' except by the Holy Spirit" (I Corinthians 12:3). If you have yielded your life to Christ, if with all your heart and mind you call him Lord, you *have* the Holy Spirit. St. John lists some other characteristics that distinguish the Spirit-indwelt person from one who is not God's child (I John, especially 4:1-3): love of other Christians and their receptivity to us; love of God and eagerness to obey his commands; freedom from continual bondage to sin. John clearly states that anyone who denies that Jesus is the Messiah of God definitely does not have God's Spirit because that Spirit is the Spirit of truth, not of error.

The exciting thing about the Holy Spirit is that, once he is inside of you, he wants to get out! He wants to manifest himself through you in every possible way. Major sections of the New Testament are devoted to gifts, supernatural empowerings of the Holy Spirit (I Corinthians 12-14; Romans 12; Ephesians 4; I Peter 4) and fruits, traits of righteousness (Galatians 5), because it is through both gifts and fruitbearing that you display the full character of God in your life and accomplish his work here on earth.

When scripture speaks of the fruit of the Spirit, it is referring to love, joy, peace, patience, kindness, goodness, faithfulness, humility, and self-control (Galatians 5:22-23). When you say "no" to your natural anger, anxiety, rebellion, general irritability, and sin, and say "yes" to the Holy Spirit, you will begin to produce the Spirit's fruit, increasingly resembling Jesus in your attitudes and disposition. "Those who belong to Christ Jesus have put to death their human nature, with all its passions and desires. The Spirit has given us life; he must also control our lives" (Galatians 5:24-25).

The gifts of the Spirit are supernatural abilities which demonstrate the power of God to heal, work miracles, instruct, and equip God's children for service. If the Christian is to be a redemptive agent of God on earth, it is essential that he be filled with the fruits of righteousness and empowered with the charisma, or supernatural empowering of God's Spirit. It is a common mistake to stress the fruits and neglect the gifts, or to place so much emphasis upon the gifts that the fruits are ignored. To be complete, mature, and effective, the Christian must seek, like Jesus, to display both.

The difference, however, is that, while *all* Christians are to manifest *all* the fruits (indeed they are commanded to do so), the gifts are distributed one here, another there as God deems best (I Corinthians 12:11).

Christians today are privileged to see an exciting resurgence of Spirit-power in the lives of ordinary believers unparalleled since the days immediately following the resurrection and ascension of Jesus Christ. Those were days of trouble and persecution and the church needed supernatural power to survive and grow. The writer of Hebrews implies that powerful demonstrations of the Holy Spirit were a foretaste of the powers of the world to come, the Kingdom Age, when all of God's children will be endowed with powers and perfection just as Jesus was. Perhaps, the contemporary manifestations of spiritual gifts are indications that troublesome days are ahead for us, and that we should look forward with eagerness to the coming of God's Kingdom in the not-too-distant future.

The following is a brief description of each of the gifts of the Spirit as they are found in Paul's writings:

Speaking in Tongues is a gift which Paul calls the "least," perhaps because it is of no public value without the sister-gift of interpretation, or because it seems to be the "beginning gift" for many. Tongues-speaking is the ability to speak a language other than your own, without understanding what is being spoken. It can be exercized at will once it has begun, but should be used aloud in public gatherings only when the Spirit directs and, then, only if there is known to be an interpreter of tongues in the congregation or group. Many Christians experience a sense of joy and delight while speaking in tongues, perhaps because it is an assurance that the Holy Spirit is within them. Indeed, it is wonderful to be able to pray or praise "in the Spirit" when you have run out of words of your own to express your love for God. If God can, thus, pray through the lips of a Christian it is an encouraging bit of spiritual equipment even though the human understanding is not benefitted by its use.

Interpretation is the ability to receive words in your own natural language from the Holy Spirit following a message in an unknown tongue. Some people with this gift actually "see" words written upon their minds; others simply receive strong impressions concerning the content of the tongues message. Everyone who speaks in tongues is told to desire the gift of interpretation as well and there are many tongues-speaking Christians who regularly interpret their own messages. There have been striking instances in the modern church of messages being delivered in unknown tongues, with interpretation afterwards, which foreigners in the congregation have been astonished to recognize as their own languages. They often attest to the accuracy of the interpretation and express surprise at learning that neither the one who gave the message nor the interpreter had ever learned the language that was spoken.

Prophecy, like interpretation, is the ability to receive from the Holy Spirit words or strong impressions which, when spoken, provide instruction, encouragement, information, prediction or loving rebuke from God for the benefit of individuals or the entire group. Paul teaches that this is one of the greatest of all the gifts and is greatly to be desired.

Wisdom and *Knowledge* are gifts which can be illustrated best by the examples Jesus himself gave us. When he was tested concerning the payment of taxes to a foreign overlord, he pointed to Caesar's head on a coin and replied, "pay to the Emperor what belongs to him, and pay to God what belongs to God" (Luke 20:25-26). This reply was so stunning in its wisdom that the men who were testing him "kept quiet, amazed at his answer." We have seen young Christians endowed with this gift give astonishingly accurate Biblical answers to difficult questions when they lacked any firsthand knowledge of such scripture themselves.

The gift of knowledge is similar, being the ability to know facts, not otherwise learned, through the inner revelation of the Spirit. When Jesus told the woman at the Samaritan well that she had five husbands it impressed her more than all the spiritual truths he had just revealed to her and she ran off and brought the entire town to hear him. This is a very awesome gift when used with love as the Spirit directs.

Discernment of Spirits is the ability to know when someone is being influenced by a spirit other than the Spirit of God. Sometimes the discerning Christian knows intuitively that a doctrine or bit of advice is coming from a demonic source; at other times this gift is strong enough to permit the Christian actually to see the evil spirit which is dominating someone. The individual with this gift must walk very carefully with the Holy Spirit and be filled with wisdom and love in order that, whenever possible, deliverence from evil spirits may be effected or their influence at least exposed and restrained.

Faith is a charismatic gift, as well as the general ability to believe in Jesus. It is the ability to believe God for great things. If a group has a need, the person gifted with faith would be the one able to claim from God the answer to that need and to trust in God without wavering.

Miracles are always needed among Christians and the Holy Spirit equips some people to perform them in order to meet the needs of the fellowship. Also, miracles are signs pointing to the power and sovereignty of God, since, wherever the gospel is preached such signs should be present to convince unbelievers and skeptics. Such miracles as the multiplication of food and the raising of the dead have occurred in recent years in Indonesian revivals and elsewhere as the Holy Spirit has poured himself out afresh upon his people.

Healing gifts are of many sorts. There are Christians able by the Spirit to heal the physical body, while others are able to restore wounded spirits and troubled minds. When a non-Christian is supernaturally healed, he is usually converted as well and his enthusiasm is so boundless that many other lives are permanently affected by his testimony.

Teaching is a gift, as well as a job, and it is a very great privilege to be taught by someone who has such a gift. It is not always to those with natural teaching ability that God gives this special gift. People with little education have often been equipped by God's Spirit with a truly miraculous ability to interpret the scriptures, speak with appropriateness and power, and have no lack of parables and examples to bring home God's message. If the churches, today, were filled with supernaturally equipped teachers, it would undoubtedly do more to increase the power and effectiveness of every member of the church than would any other single gift.

Apostles were a gift to the church. Today, we might call them missionaries. These are men and women called and equipped by the Spirit to endure the rigors of living abroad in order to preach the word of God with love and power in foreign lands. There may be no more difficult calling within the church. It is of benefit to us who remain behind because it provides us with the opportunity to give and pray to help others.

Pastors are Christians to whom God has given the special responsibility of shepherding or caring for the needs of other Christians in a community. Pastors must be equipped, well and truly, with love, wisdom, and patience · if they are to shepherd other Christians and give counsel and advice as God leads.

Evangelists are those who have the charismatic ability to preach the word of truth with such convincing power that nonbelievers are converted.

Administrators are essential to any organization not only to oversee the business details but, in the Christian community, to recognize the diversity of gifts among the entire membership and order them, under God, to function harmoniously together. The ability to administer finances and organize people is of great worth and requires excessive tact. There is a sad lack in Christians groups today of those with this gift.

Helps are absolutely essential to any group. God has seen fit to give some people a supernatural calling and ability to spot areas where help is needed and to offer their assistance without reluctance. The ability to desire such jobs and do them faithfully without resentment or complaint—often without pay—is indeed a supernatural gift.

These gifts are not to be confused with psychic powers. The Holy Spirit never relies on crystal balls or other means of divination. When the charismatic gifts of the Spirit are functioning, the human mind is never passive, there is no emotional or physical manipulation, no peculiar bodily sensations in the Christian through whom He is working. The Holy Spirit never forces a child of God to do anything. So-called psychic gifts which have been present since childhood are not to be confused with the gifts of the Holy Spirit of God which can only be manifested in a truly committed Christian.

Paul makes it clear that the Holy Spirit gives his gifts for one reason: upbuilding and encouraging the entire Christian community and converting non-Christians to Christ. You may be greatly blessed when you receive a gift from the Spirit, but your being personally blessed is not, primarily, what the Spirit has in mind when he gives you his gifts. He is thinking of your brothers and sisters in Christ who need what you can now supply. It is extremely important that you and I maintain this perspective. There is a dangerous tendency in groups in which charismatic gifts are manifested for persons having them to be proud, condescending, or critical, and to make those who don't, feel jealous, suspicious, accusing, and burdened with a sense of inadequacy. Nowhere in scripture is there any indication that the Holy Spirit bestows gifts according to merit or spiritual progress. Gifts are given at the discretion of the Holy Spirit, sometimes to very young Christians who need the help of older brothers and sisters who do not happen to have that, or any discernible, gift. You must be very careful never to make a fellow Christian feel less useful or devoted because his gifts differ from your own.

An entire chapter in I Corinthians is devoted to the attitude which must distinguish a gifted Christian. Paul makes it very clear that unless you are filled with love and compassion, your gifts will never be used properly (I Corinthians 13). We have heard Christians say, "he may speak in tongues, but he certainly doesn't behave much like a Christian," and, with that observation, their interest in spiritual gifts was slackened. You are to "make love your aim, and earnestly desire the spiritual gifts" (I Corinthians 14:1 RSV). If you are seeking gifts, you had better be seeking love as well. There is scriptural evidence that love and compassion must be stirred within you if you are to use any of the healing gifts effectively. If you are constantly seeking love as the dominant quality in your life, you will not become proud of your gifts, nor will you be filled with jealousy or despair because you have not yet been given your gifts.

How do you receive the Holy Spirit's gifts? There is no single answer to this question. Sometimes they just appear; sometimes there is prolonged seeking and preparation before a gift is appropriated. Occasionally, a need is so great that the Christian simply asks for the gift he needs, claims it in faith, and trusts that he has it. Frequently, gifts are transmitted through the laying-on-of-hands. There would seem to be two factors which are usually present when gifts are given: need and desire. They work together because where there is a need, there is certainly a desire to have that need met. You may have a burning desire for a gift, without there being an evident need for it. The desire may be from God and, once the gift is received, the need it was intended to meet will become evident.

It is possible to desire spiritual gifts for the wrong reasons—carnal ambition or the desire to impress others. It is possible to have a legitimate Spirit-given hunger for a gift and yet be driven to despair and frustration because the Spirit seems reluctant to give the gift. This emotional confusion may be hindering the Spirit. If you are distraught with unfulfilled yearning, let it go, and put it into the Spirit's hands, forget about it for awhile.

In most instances in which gifts are being sought, the pattern is as follows: the Holy Spirit will lead you to people or literature where the gifts are discussed. This is usually followed by a time of preparation when questions are asked and answered, stumbling blocks removed, and experiences given which bring you into the place where you are able to receive the gift. Then, usually, there is a time of waiting upon the Lord, learning patience and faith, before you are given the gifts you have been seeking.

Practice is essential. "What you don't use, you lose." I know of very few effective Christians who were simply "zapped." Whether your gift is soul-winning, preaching, administering a church or fellowship group, speaking in tongues, or whatever, faithful use of what God gives leads to real ministry; waiting for God to do it all himself doesn't. Remember the parable of the talents.

Sometimes God surprises his children and, suddenly, bestows on them gifts which they find hard to understand and had not been seeking. This, however, is the exception and not the rule. The Spirit wants you to be able to use your gifts wisely, carefully, so that no reproach will fall upon you. It is important that you realize this, and be cautious about encouraging other Christians to plunge into the search for charismatic gifts before the Holy Spirit has prepared them. It is possible to "play God" in this matter. You must remember that the gifts are the Spirit's, not yours, to distribute.

As a Christian, you can hope for continual experiences of the Holy Spirit, greater gifts and deeper fruit, because your relationship with this mysterious and marvelous Person is never static, never limited, never finalized. St. Paul tells you to "keep on being filled with the Spirit" (Ephesians 5:18 rendered from the Greek). Jesus said, "how much more, then, the Father in heaven will give the Holy Spirit to those who ask him!" (Luke 11:13). In most places in which the word "gift" is used in the New Testament it does not refer to the specific charismatic gifts given by the Spirit but to the Holy Spirit himself, God's great gift to man. Seek the Spirit, and, as you let him have his way with you, he will give you the gifts and ministries that you desire and much more. If you hunger for the Giver more than the gifts you shall never be disappointed.

 ## 19 *The Return of Jesus Christ: The Point of Everything*

CHRISTIANITY IS a religion of wonderful anticipation and the central feature of that anticipation is the return of Jesus Christ—the real, physical, touch-me-and-see, personal return of the same Lord who walked in Galilee 2,000 years ago.

Jesus said that he would come back and that people everywhere would see (and recognize) him with their own eyes. He will come with all the might and majesty of God and there will be no mistaking who he is. He will come again for those who have him in their hearts (by the Holy Spirit) and for those who do not. He will come when most men aren't expecting it in the least, "like a thief in the night" (Luke 12:39, also I Thessalonians 5:2).

There will be those who are angered at his coming, although almost everyone has always suspected that sometime, somehow, God would have to intervene in history and call a halt to the oppression, corruption, and sin of the world. No just, or loving, God would endlessly endure the evil and rebellion of his creation without eventually stepping in to set things right. How better to do so than by sending his Son unexpectedly with great power and authority? Who should be better able to judge us and set our world right than One who lived among men and tasted both the joy and suffering of human existence? Who else knows human hearts so well? Who else knows what it will take to remake the earth, so that it may be once again a paradise exactly suited to the needs and desires of mankind.

The Jews of Jesus' day wanted all that. They earnestly yearned for a King who would right all wrongs—especially those committed against *them!*, punish the wicked—mainly *their* enemies, and elevate his faithful people to a position of preeminence in a Heaven on earth.

In fact, so great was their expectation, and so well-founded on ancient prophetic utterances, that Jesus was hard put to convince them that, while that day *would* come, the time was not yet. His initial ministry was not one of judgment. God wanted to win men by loving them, if he could. However, his "courtship" of men was not to go on forever. When men have been given ample opportunity to choose him freely, and have put his laws into practice, he will return, whether they have done so or not. On that day there will be no more time for "freely choosing." On that day Jesus will come as Judge and will establish himself as King (I Thessalonians 5:13).

2,000 years ago, God's hand was outstretched in love to his wayward children. Soon, perhaps, you and I will see his hand upheld in judgment against those who do not love, listen to, or obey him. Finally we will thrill to see God's hand at work in re-creation. Always, in all things pertaining to men, God works through a Man, his Son, our Saviour, Judge, and King (Philippians 2:5-11).

It is easy, and appropriate, to be in awe of this. But we are not meant to be frightened by it. In judging, God does not change his character; even his judgment is wrapped in love. The disciples, who were just as awestruck by it all as we, encourage us to be excited, enthusiastic, and expectant about it—for them it really was the point of everyhing.

When you became a Christian, you could have spoken about it in two different ways, each way emphasizing a separate aspect of your conversion. You could have said, "I have finished with the old life, the sinful, selfish ways— they have been judged, sentenced, and done away with." Or, you could have said, "I have begun a new, wonderful life, lived with God, and it's the most fantastic experience I ever dreamed of!"

You would be right in both cases. The first description centers on what you have been saved *from;* the second on what you are being saved *for.*

It is thus with the second coming of Christ. He spoke of it as "the end" and "the judgment"—but also as a "birth," of which the judgment is only a prelude. Ends and deaths *are* rather frightening; but births are thrilling. Both of them are essential to life, and, for most of us, every truly meaningful experience is both a dying and a being born; the passing of something outdated and inadequate; the beginning of something relevant and significant. Christ's return is frightening because it means the end of everything as you know it and the judgment of all that you are. But it is exciting because it heralds a new age, the dawn of a world where righteousness, justice, and love—so longed for, yet so elusive—are as real and plentiful as rivers and mountains (*cf.* Revelation 21, 22).

Most of us, when we think of Christ's return, tend to think only of the judgment we will receive. It is sobering, but important for us to do this, but not to dwell on it so overly much that we fail to glimpse what it leads to.

You and I shall be examined by One who cannot be fooled, One who knows each word we have spoken and every thought we have held. No mistakes will be made, no error of evaluation; it will be absolutely perfect judgment. All hiding, all sham, all self-justification will fall away. It will be a relief; or a terror. It will heal unto life eternal; or hurt unto everlasting death. As C. S. Lewis has said,

We shall not only believe, we shall know, know beyond doubt in every fibre of our appalled or delighted being, that as the Judge has said, so we are; neither more nor less nor other. We shall perhaps even realize that in some dim fashion we could have known it all along. We shall know and all creation will know too: our ancestors, our parents, our wives or husbands, our children. The unanswerable and (by then) self-evident truth about each will be known to all.[1]

The apostle John said there are two reactions men will have on the day of judgment: "remain in him, so that we may be *full of courage* when he appears and need not *hide in shame* from him on the Day he comes." (I John 2:28 [italics ours]) Your reaction to his coming is itself a kind of judgment. If you "hide in shame" it is because you are among those who have refused him your obedience. If you welcome him, "full of courage," it is because you know that you have tried with diligence to serve him because you love him. If you "remain in him" and treasure your relationship to Christ above all else, you will rejoice at his return, and your joy will be the sure evidence that your judgment will be gentle and end in eternal life beside your Lord.

The really important thing, however, is what lies beyond the judgment. Perhaps, if you would let your mind dwell more often on the new age to come and less upon the end of this one, you would find deep comfort in the thought of your Lord's return. For your God is not a God who cares only about the salvation of individual men, he cares about societies, organizations, governments, and the creation itself: the birds of the air, the lilies of the field, the hairs of your head, and every other aspect of this teeming world. All of it needs redemption; all will be redeemed. The combined utopias of all the ages cannot begin to approach the wonder of the Kingdom age to come. Those utopias were limited by the weakness of the men who conceived them and tried to carry them out. Somebody said, "you won't restore a house that's rotted out by rearranging its timbers; you'll restore it by replacing them" (*cf.* I Corinthians 3:12-15).

In the Kingdom of God, the evil forces which cause you to fail and fall will be bound, your mind will be freed from fear and ignorance, and all of the secret laws of this universe will be unlocked for your benefit. Most wonderful of all will be the joy of serving Christ, being an active co-worker with him in the task of reclaiming a polluted, war-torn world. That's the promise made to those who love and obey Jesus—that this life is largely a training period for that time when Christians shall be entrusted with the responsibility of administering his love and his law in the new creation (*cf.* Luke 19:11-17).

The notion of a glorious new age is easily ridiculed because so many have dared to hope for it only to have it delayed. And the thought that it might come suddenly, through divine intervention, disturbs the assumption that change is gradual, the result of a long evolutionary process. It is discomforting—at the least—to think of the curtain dropping on *your* important little play, the lightning striking so abruptly when *you* had such marvelous things yet to do. If utopia is to come, *you* want to bring it in!

Maybe that's why God plans it differently. He wants to find you as you really are, doing what you normally do, because on that day all playacting will cease and Reality will illuminate all things.

Perhaps his delay is because he loves you and wants you to be ready. God knows you well enough to know that you would probably *not* be ready if you could pinpoint his coming because real readiness consists of obedient daily living. If you don't know the exact hour he's coming, you must be ready *always*. Unless you begin *now* preparing for that day you won't be ready at all.

Jesus didn't leave you completely in the dark. He knew the difficulty of living in a state of continual anticipation, so he shared with his loved ones all he knew concerning the signs of his coming. (The study guide for this chapter deals with some of these—they're exciting.) Are we approaching that time? Be careful not to be overly certain that yours is to be the final generation, for others have thought so before and have brought the gospel into disrepute by premature predictions. But, look about you—"watch" said Jesus and so many of the New Testament writers. The day *must* come, it *is* coming, and, perhaps, soon.

Don't be fearful. No one who is Christ's will be lost. Abide in him and take your relationship with him with utmost seriousness. Think of his coming with joy; let it be a sweet hope to help you set your mind on the things of God and put his service first in your life. "He who gives his testimony to all this says, 'Certainly so! I am coming soon!' So be it. Come, Lord Jesus. May the grace of the Lord Jesus be with all" (Revelation 22:20-21).

NOTES
[1] Lewis, C. S., *The World's Last Night*. New York: Harcourt, Brace & World, 1960, page 113.

Suggestions
for Study

1. Introduction: What Is a Christian?

The Bible offers information about what a Christian is and how one becomes a Christian. Basically, this information can be summarized as follows: You must *believe* that Jesus is God and that, by his death, your sins have been forgiven and you are God's child. You must *experience* God's Spirit in your heart, giving you an inner assurance that God loves and accepts you and filling you with a love for Jesus, other people, and especially, fellow Christians. God will not be real to you if you have only belief without some experience of the Spirit. You must *do* certain things: hunger to obey God's Spirit; please him in your daily life; hate sin and resist it in your own life; abide in God's word, loving it, trying always to learn and apply it in your everyday experiences.

Following is a questionnaire which might help you if you have some question about your relationship to God:

1. Do you believe, with head and heart, that Jesus came in the flesh as God's chosen savior?

2. Do you know that all your sins have been forgiven through Jesus and that you are now made right (reconciled) to God?

3. Do you believe that you are saved, not by your own efforts or good works, but by the grace and mercy of God?

4. Do you know that you have eternal life?

5. Have you asked Jesus to enter your life by his Spirit?

6. Have you experienced his Holy Spirit in your heart?

7. If not, have you asked God to send his Spirit into your heart on the basis of the promises given in Luke 11:5-13?

8. Do you love other Christians?

9. Are you striving to be obedient to God and to please him in every aspect of your life?

10. Are you trying to learn the Bible, reading it daily as often as you can, and trying to live according to its guidelines?

11. Are you willing to tell others that you believe in Jesus?

If you can answer "yes" to the above questions, then you can be confident that you are a Christian. If you can answer "yes," but still have a lingering doubt in your mind, you may have sins in your life you have not confessed and forsaken. Tell God about it; ask for his forgiveness and help.

2. Start with the Bible

One of the Bible's most important statements about itself is to be found in II Tim 3:14-17.

1. What, according to this passage, are the Holy Scriptures useful for? Think of examples in the Bible or in your own experience in which Scripture has been used for each of the functions Paul enumerates.

2. What is the difference between knowing the truth and living it? How has the truth "liberated" you? See John 8:32.

3. Read some Christian biographies (available at Christian bookstores in inexpensive paperback). Discuss the role of the Bible in the lives of the great Christian men and women described.

4. In prayer, ask God how your attitude towards the Bible may be improved. Ask him to show you how you can spend more time each day studying his Word.

5. Begin memorizing scripture, a verse every day, in order to plant God's truth deep in your mind.

3. For More Effective Prayer

1. Read II Chron 20:1-30. What prayer principles are illustrated here? What does Jehoshaphat do besides pray? Examine his prayer carefully. At what point does he get down to his own problems? What is his attitude towards God as he prays?

2. Study Daniel 6. What role did prayer play in Daniel's life? What could be the effect on others of our faithfulness in daily prayer? How would you react in Daniel's situation? Has it ever "cost" you anything to be a Christian?

3. Every prayer should involve:
   a) praise to God, for himself and for what he has done in Christ;
   b) confession of known sins and request for pardon;
   c) thanksgiving for pardon received and for other blessings;

d) intercession for the needs of others;

e) petition for your own needs.

If you have a prayer group, form a circle and have a few minutes of spontaneous, one-sentence prayers in each of these categories.

4. Some suggested passages for study or discussion might include: Matt 6:5-15; Matt 7:7-11; Phil 4:6-7; II Chron 7:14; Ps 145:18.

5. A prayer diary is helpful. Keep a brief record of your daily prayers, describing alongside each prayer how much real faith you have for that particular request as well as any guidance given you by the Holy Spirit as you thought and prayed about the matter. As days go by, your request may change, be renounced, or be encouraged and answered. Do this for at least three months, then reread it, asking God to show you what you need to learn about prayer.

4. Guidance: How to Hear God Speaking

1. Read Gideon's story in Judges 6 and 7. What was Gideon like? What do we learn about God from this passage? How did God guide Gideon?

2. Study the ways God guided the early church in Acts 1; 5; 10; 21.

3. Read Acts 16 and Acts 27-28. What effect does suffering have on the disciples? Why? How does Paul view circumstances?

4. Read Luke 1-2, looking for the ways in which God engineered circumstances, gave guidance, controlled events, gave signs, spoke through scripture and mature Christians, and gave miracles.

5. In your fellowship group, share with each other ways in which you have been guided in your decision-making or ways in which, although God's guidance was not apparent at the time of decision, his hand was apparent in the outcome.

5. How Far Should I Go With Sex?

1. Matt 6:19-34 doesn't refer to sex directly but it does raise several issues applicable to it. Read it and consider the following:

a) What pressures affect my social (dating) life? How do I respond to them?

b) What promises of God apply to my needs? Note that this includes all needs, even sexual.

c) Where is my "treasure"? Where does it appear to be judging from the way I behave, the way I talk with other people, and the way I think when I am alone?

d) One translation reads "if thine eye be single, thy whole body shall be full of light." What is the singleness of vision being spoken of? What is the danger of double vision?

e) What "masters" do I serve?

2. The Old Testament reveals God's attitude towards sexual sins. Read Deut 22:13-30. Divide the passage as follows, asking in each section what sexual condition is being described, how it can be applied to our culture, and what God thinks about it: vss. 13-19; 20-21; 22; 23-27; 28-29.

3. For New Testament scriptures dealing with sexual behavior, study I Cor 6:15-20 and I Cor 7:1-2.

6. Drugs and Drink

1. Study Rom 14:21. What is a right motive for abstinence? What does "stumble" mean? Who is your "brother"?

2. Read Romans 13, Titus 3, and I Peter 2. Discuss the youth culture's scorn for such concepts as these. How do adults regard them? Why? If people disregard civil authority, what authority do they, in fact, regard?

3. Read Is 5:11-25. What does God think about those who do such things? What does our culture think? If our attitude as Christians is to be like God's, how should we feel when we see such things? What can we do about them?

4. In your fellowship group, have role-playing sessions in which one person is a Christian, one is a non-Christian who is open to Christianity, and one is an unconverted agnostic. Have each actor react in the way he feels the individual he is characterizing would react to drinking, drugs, sex, *etc*. How can the Christian present more effectively and lovingly his (the Biblical) point of view? How can Christians abstain from drugs and drink without alienating peers or tactlessly condemning parents?

5. Discuss why it is difficult to say "no" when it comes to drink or drugs. Why do people take drinks or drugs? Why do they often

resent those who do not? The issues are usually those of fear, insecurity, the need for approval. Wherein does the Christian's security lie? Whose condemnation does he fear? Whose approval does he seek?

7. The Occult

1. The Old Testament reveals God's attitude towards sorcery and the black arts. Examine the following references to get a complete picture of God's viewpoint; God's laws are the same today as they were when the verses were written: Ex 22:18; Lev 19:26-28; Deut 13:1-5; and 18:9-14; I Sam 15:23; Is 8:19; Mal 3:5; and Mic 3:7.

2. There is an account of necromancy in I Sam 28:3-20. Why did Saul seek a medium? Verse 18 gives one reason why God refused to answer Saul. Why is the medium so astonished in verse 12? (Many Christians are convinced that mediums never really contact the spirits of dead human beings, but only evil spirits who knew and can imitate the dead person. This could explain the witch's surprise at seeing Samuel's spirit.) How does Samuel treat Saul? What is Saul's reaction to the encounter?

3. Read the Book of Acts in the New Testament and note the following references to the black arts:

   a) *Acts 8:9-13* Why was Simon amazed?

   b) *Acts 13:8-12* From where does the greater power come? What is the source of Elymas' power? What is the result of Paul's dealings with Elymas?

   c) *Acts 16:16-24* What is the motive behind the owners of the slave girl? Why was Paul in Philippi? What does this teach us about the motive behind much of today's occult activity? What was the source of the slave girl's powers? What charge is brought against Paul and Silas in verse 21? Whenever Christians "advocate customs" pleasing to God, there is a conflict. Why did Paul wait many days before casting out the divining spirit?

   d) *Acts 19:13-20* What is necessary before a person can deal successfully with evil spirits? What did the Holy Spirit motivate the new Christians to do (verses 18-19)? What was the result?

4. Suggested reading:

The Challenging Counterfeit, Raphael Gasson (Logos, 1966).

Defeated Enemies, Corrie Ten Boom (Christian Literature Crusade, 1962).

Biblical Demonology, Merrill F. Unger (Scripture Press, 1952).

Satan is Alive and Well on Planet Earth, Hal Lindsey (Zondervan, 1972).

Angels of Light, Hobart Freeman (Logos, 1969).

War on the Saints, Jesse Penn-Lewis (Christian Literature Crusade, 1964).

8. *What is Christian Fellowship?*

1. Read Rev 2:1 to 3:22. List everything that the Lord condemns and everything he praises. Does your group fit any of these descriptions?

2. Read and study Acts 1 and 2 noting the ways in which the members of the early church interacted; handled problems; discovered God's will; related to outsiders; met their basic needs.

3. What things does Jesus pray for in Jn 17?

4. Study Jn 15. What marks a disciple? How do we remain in the Father's love? What marks Jesus' friends? How is the world going to view and treat us? Why?

5. Read the following passages in I and II Cor:

I Cor 1:10-31; 3-6; 12:12-31; 13; 14; 16.

II Cor 2; 6; 8; 12:19-21; 13.

What principles did Paul lay down for the Christians at Corinth? What were some of their problems? How do they compare with problems in your fellowship group or church? Note the way Paul suggests we relate to other Christians as well as non-Christians.

9. *How to Share Your Faith*

1. The Bible has many examples of men and women who were good witnesses. Hebrews 11 names some of them. Studies of people such as Moses, Daniel, and Paul will be helpful in understanding your own opportunity for witness. Regarding any of these figures, ask yourself:

a) What made him stand out against his historical setting? What problem or blessing made him different from others around him?

b) What effect on others did his involvement in the things of God have? What kinds of conflict did it lead to?

c) Did he represent adequately the truth in that situation? What was the result of his witness? Can we learn from him?

Beyond such questions, we may speculate on the motivations of characters in a story. For example, look at the story of Jesus healing a blind man in Jn 9.

a) What was the real concern of the Pharisees? Why were they threatened? How might God's reality in your life become a threat to others?

b) What was the man's source of boldness? How did his refusal to discuss irrelevancies contribute to this?

c) What presuppositions were overthrown in this episode? What opinions had to be questioned?

d) How are God's purposes served when we are faithful to tell what he has done, *regardless of the effect on others*?

10. How Can I Relate to My Parents?

1. Look up the following Old Testament passages to get an idea of how strongly God rebuked children who disregarded their obligations to their parents: Ex 21:15, 17; Lev 20:9; Deut 21:18-21.

2. How do you think the future generations would be affected if one generation began to live up to God's standards for their relations to their parents? How would the parents themselves be affected?

3. Study Paul's instructions in Col 3:12-25. Characterize the attitudes he urges on each category of people. How is his teaching different from the contemporary approach?

4. What is the relationship between living out the instructions of God with other people and belief that the Lord himself is involved in all of our activity (Col 3:23-25)?

5. The book of Proverbs gives strong advice to those whose concern it is to know God's opinion in this area. Read it, willing to obey, and ask God for the strength to do so.

11. Fear and Depression: How to Cope

1. Read the book of Psalms through at least once with a will to obey the Holy Spirit as He speaks to you about letting go of your fears. Don't fight with the injunction to trust in God—do it!

2. Having read the entire book, select ten Psalms you would give to a depressed or anxious person to read. Why did you select them?

3. Write down any unforgiven sins in your life that you have either failed to acknowledge, or refused to give up. Note, especially, sins of anger, resentment, and jealousy. Write them down, believing you are giving them to God and he is tearing them up and throwing them away. Cross each off when you can truly believe yourself forgiven on the basis of I Jn 1:9.

4. You can't say "can't." Read I Cor 10:13. You are not allowed to think that your case is special or impossibly difficult. What "way out" is available to you in your specific case? God will show you. Now read I Cor 10:12. Where does your ability to cope come from?

5. Read Foxe's *Book of Martyrs* (Revell, 1968), available in paperback. It will help you get your own problems into perspective and encourage your faith in God's ability to help you.

6. Study Ps 106 after reading Heb 3:7-19. Why, according to Hebrews, were the Israelites unable to enter into the promised land? In Ps 106, list every sin which Israel committed during its wilderness journey. These same sins may be preventing you from entering into a free and victorious life.

7. Read Num 13:17-14:36. Why were the people unwilling to enter the promised land when God wanted them to? Compare the attitudes of Joshua and Caleb to the attitudes of the other spies. What report would you believe? How does God view fear? Why was he angry with the people for being afraid? What should they have been? Is fear keeping you from God's promises and provisions? Read Josh 1:1-9.

8. Depression can result from laziness, irresponsibility, chronic lateness, and procrastination because these cause guilt which is a major factor behind most depression. These sins cause you to hurt people, fail at your work, and disappoint yourself. How do you handle it when you do these things? Do you make excuses for

yourself? Do you get angry when you are expected to be responsible? By confessing, being truly sorry, and apologizing to those
whom you have hurt or disappointed, you can begin to discipline
yourself and get rid of potential guilt and depression. Be honest
with God, others, and yourself. These "traits" mentioned above are
sins, and must be dealt with as such.

12. Why do I Keep Sinning, What can I do about it?

1. A study of sin must always be balanced by a study of God's
grace. Read the following passages for a balanced view of both
aspects of God's truth:

  a) We are saved by faith, not good works: Heb 11, Gal 3
  and 5; Jn 3:14-18; Eph 2:1-10 and 4.
  b) We must strive for righteousness and holiness if we are
  to become like Jesus: II Pet 3; I Cor 5 and 6:7-20; Matt
  7:21-27; Jam 2:14-26.
  c) Contrasting studies might be made of Heb 11 and 12; Jam
  2 and Heb 11; Gal 5 and Eph 5; I Jn 1 and I Jn 3:1-10.

2. For a New Testament account of man's sin and God's response, make a study of Rom 1 and 3. Why does Paul say man
sins? How are sinners made righteous?

3. In the Old Testament, study Genesis 3, asking: Why did
Eve give in? What did the serpent want? What might "death"
mean? How do Adam and Eve react when confronted with their
sin? How should they have responded? (Read I Jn 1:9.) Why is
Adam's sin in v. 17 so serious? How does sin affect the relationship
between Adam and Eve? Study Rom 5:12-18 for the consequences
of Adam's fall and God's solution.

4. How do you react to your own sin? Read how Judas tried
to cope with sin in Matt 26:14-15; 47-56; 27:1-10. What chances
did he have to repent? How did he respond to Christ's continued
affection? Read about Peter's sin and repentance: Matt 26:30-35;
36-46; 57-75. Now read Jn 21. Peter repented; Judas despised
himself. How does Peter respond when given another chance to
see Jesus in Jn 21-7? How does Jesus treat Peter's desire for a
restored relationship? Did he leave any room for Peter to express
discouragement or to make explanations or justifications?

13. Can I Believe What I Read in the Bible?

Study the gospels and note how frequently Jesus uses the Scriptures in his conversations and his preaching. He submitted himself continually to their authority. Similarly, note how frequently the writers of the epistles quote the Scriptures.

Read Psalm 119. What does this psalm teach about the Word of God, and the appropriate attitude of men to that Word?

Some of the following books may be of real worth to you as you investigate further the question of Biblical authority:

Albright, W. F. *The Archaeology of Palestine* (Penguin, 1956).

—————. *Recent Discoveries in Bible Lands* (Funk & Wagnall, 1955).

Bruce, F. F., ed. *The New Testament Documents: Are They Reliable* (Eerdmans, 1959).

Douglas, J. D., ed. *The New Bible Dictionary* (Eerdmans, 1962).

Guthrie, Donald, ed. *The Revised New Bible Commentary* (Eerdmans, 1970).

—————. *New Testament Introduction*, rev. ed. (Inter-Varsity Press, 1971).

Henry, Carl F., ed. *Revelation and the Bible*, 4th ed. (Baker Book House, 1967).

Johnson, Douglas. *The Christian and His Bible* (Inter-Varsity Press, 1962).

Kenyon, Sir Frederic G. *Our Bible and The Ancient Manuscripts* (London: Eyre and Spottiswoode, 1941).

Packer, James I. *Fundamentalism and the Word of God* (Eerdmans, 1958).

Short, A. Rendle. *Archaeology Gives Evidence* (Tyndale Press, 1951).

Young, E. J. *An Introduction to the Old Testament*, rev. ed. (Eerdmans, 1958).

14. The Trinity

The Old Testament is full of hints about what the Messiah would be like when, at last, he arrived. It also has some remarkable things to say about the Holy Spirit. Some of the most important passages are these

1. *Psalm 22.* Possibly written by David, this Psalm goes far beyond anything that David himself ever experienced. It describes the crucifixion of Jesus in surprising detail, though it was written 1,000 years before he lived. Does this Psalm add to your understanding of Jesus' agonized cry from the cross (Matt 27:46)? Do you find any support in Psalm 22 for the view that on the cross Jesus doubted God? Why could the Psalm not be about David, or any historical individual other than Jesus? Note verse 13 especially. How many specific references to the events of Good Friday can you find there?

2. *Isaiah 52:13-53:12.* Again, we have a predictive prophecy, written in the past tense about 750 years before Christ. One suspects that the prophet "saw" a vision of some sort concerning the One he describes and that the past tense is used because he is literally recounting what he saw during that revelation. In what ways does this passage predict not only the crucifixion but the resurrection? In chapter 52, verse 13-15, there is an important contrast between one kind of astonishment and another on the parts of kings and nations. What is this contrast? How does this promise of chapter 52 go beyond even resurrection?

3. *Ezekiel 34.* Written around 600 B.C., everything in this chapter is said of God himself, with one important exception. Although David had been dead for nearly 400 years, verse 23 says "I will set up over then . my servant David." (It was common to use the name of a man's ancestor in speaking of him if the ancestor was also an important figure.) Who is the servant referred to in verses 23 and 24? What are the distinctions made in these verses between God and his servant who is to come? How does this distinction break down in verses 11-15 and verse 31? How can God and his "servant" be the same?

4. *Jeremiah 31:31-34.* What are the contrasts between the two covenants spoken of here? What is necessary for the second that was not part of the first? Does Joel 2:28-29 explain this?

5. Compare Jn 1:1-18, which is basically philosophical, with Heb 1 and 2, which is basically taken from the Old Testament, to see the way in which the apostles saw Jesus as the fulfillment of everything the Old Covenant was really about. Yet, by fulfilling it they maintained that he ushered in something altogether new

How did John and the author of Hebrews understand the human Jesus to fit into the eternal scheme of God's plan? What was God like before Jesus was born?

15. The Work of Christ

1. Re-read the parable of the Prodigal Son in Luke 15. Identify the characters in it. How does the elder son typify Jesus? differ from him? What insights can you draw about the cost of reconciliation? The inheritance having already been divided, who owned all the things used to celebrate the prodigal's return? What can we learn of God's attitude toward sinners? What is the prerequisite to being accepted after having "left home"?

2. In Col 1, we glimpse the magnitude of "at-one-ment" accomplished in Christ.

   a) List all the specific things said about him.
   b) How is his accomplishment dependent upon who he is?
   c) What part does your faith play in reconciliation?
   d) How does this passage expand your view of the human Jesus?

3. As you may gather from the Biblical references in it, the book of Hebrews is largely devoted to the question of how the work of Christ relates to all that preceded it in the Old Testament. Study especially chapters 5 and 10.

   a) Look for all the points of similarity and difference between the priests of the Old Testament and our "high priest," Jesus.
   b) What can you discover about the strange figure Melchizedek? See Gen 14:17-20 and Ps 110:4. A common Hebrew belief was that one could never be superior to one's parents inasmuch as everything one is, biologically, is inherited from them. What bearing does this have on both the passage in Genesis and that in Ps 110?

5. An excellent project would be to outline this chapter. Look up Bible verses that bear upon it and spend some time thinking of how you might follow this basic pattern when sharing Christianity with your friends. After studying this chapter, can you prepare a summary of the gospel, with supportive scripture, in your own words? To share with a friend how you became a Christian

is only an "appetizer"; the "main course" is to explain to him simply, clearly and with love, what Jesus did for him.

16. What About All Those Who Haven't Heard of Christ?

Study Romans 1 with some care. It is a tightly-organized argument that is gaining support from modern anthropology. We have never found a people, no matter how primitive, that did not believe a) in the Golden Rule—that we ought to do unto others as we want them to do to us—and, b) that behind the Golden Rule stands a creator to whom we are responsible.

A hundred years ago it was said commonly that the belief in one creator-god developed slowly; that first came superstition based on fear, then polytheism (the worship of many gods) and magic, and then, finally, monotheism (belief in one god) appeared. Modern study has reversed this view and shown that Paul was on the right track: belief in one God came first. The belief in many gods and the use of magic was a *degeneration* from this.

1. What does Paul say, in Rom 1, that all men necessarily know about God?

2. What implication does he draw about the justice of God from this fact?

3. What is the relationship between our moral responsibility to God and our intellectual understanding of him?

4. Read chapter 2, especially verses 12-16. What does it mean to be "righteous through faith"?—Look back to 1:17. The Jew has faith in the God of Israel, in the Old Testament, in the Law. What does the Gentile have faith in?

5. What does it mean to be a "doer of the Law" and not a "hearer" only? (Rom 2:13). See also Jam 1 : 2

17. How Can a Good God Allow Suffering?

Although we have referred repeatedly in this chapter to passages in the book of Romans, a careful study of Rom 5-8 would be valuable because these chapters summarize the Christian view of suffering as well as the Christian view of sin.

Although the book of Job argues strongly against the idea that sickness was a punishment for specific sins, many Jews believed that sin and suffering were connected. In Romans, Paul says that there is a connection between sickness (and other suffering) and sin, although it is not on a one-to-one basis. Read Rom 5-8 and consider:

1. What is the connection as Paul sees it?

2. To what part of us does sin, sickness, and death pertain?

3. What changes the picture for the Christian? That is, what is added to the old self to make it a new self?

4. If we continue to sin, yet it is not really us (see Rom 7), is there a parallel to be drawn in that we continue to suffer, yet it is not really us? (Read 1 Pet 4:13). Can it be argued that we die, but it is not really us? (See Jn 11:26).

5. Note: Paul does not say we rejoice in the midst of suffering. He says we rejoice in the suffering itself! What is the key to this? (Rom 5:5).

18. The Holy Spirit and His Gifts

1. Read Acts and underline every reference to the Holy Spirit. Keep a notebook listing every reference and what it teaches you about the Holy Spirit.

2. Read Luke 1-3, noting the references to the Holy Spirit. What signs and wonders did the Spirit perform in connection with the birth of Jesus?

3. Study the following passages and note the things that result from the Holy Spirit's activity: II Chron 20:13-17; Is 61:1; 11:2-5; Ezek 36:27; Mic 3:8; Zech 4:6; Joel 2:28-29; Is 59:19; II Pet 1:21; Mark 16:15-19; Luke 12:12; John 14:26; Matt 12:28; John 7:38-39; II Cor 3:17; Acts 4:31; I Cor 2:4; Acts 10:19-20; 13:2-4.

4. Carefully study Luke 11:5-13. What promises are given? What are the pictures of God in this section? Why did Jesus choose these to illustrate his point? What is our role in receiving the Holy Spirit more abundantly? Is there any indication that this is a gift we receive once and for all?

5. Any of the following passages would make excellent studies on the Holy Spirit: Jn 14:12-31; Rom 8; Jn 15:26-16:15.

6. Begin to pray daily for more of God's Spirit. Ask him to put

into your heart a hunger for the spiritual gifts he wishes you to have. If you already have some gifts, ask God to increase your boldness in their public use and train you to listen more sensitively to the Spirit's leading in their use.

7. If you have a prayer or fellowship group, study the gifts of the Spirit and discuss what it would mean if such gifts were manifested in your midst. Be very honest. How would you feel if your pastor, your parents, your friends, or, if you are married, your marriage partner, began to use charismatic gifts? What would be the effect on your parish of a healing service? If there is fear, distrust, concern, doubt, or puzzlement among you, discuss it and try to bring every member into the Biblical perspective.

19. The Return of Jesus Christ: The Point of Everything

Jesus discussed his return most explicitly in a sermon recorded in Matt 24, Mark 13, and Luke 21. Read these accounts and draw up a list of all the specific "signs" which Jesus said would herald his coming. One of the most exciting studies you can make is to discover all you can about each of these in terms of our own current events.

1. Make a graph showing the extent and intensity of armed warfare throughout recorded history.

2. What is the extent of persecution and martyrdom of Christians and Jews in this century? When did it peak?

3. What would you say are the "false Messiahs" proclaimed today?

4. How near to the evangelization of the whole world are we? (You might write to the American Bible Society at 1865 Broadway, New York, N. Y. 10023 for information on this one.) Does Jesus say that every *person* will hear the gospel before he comes?

5. Read Daniel for what information there is on the "desolating sacrilege" and check a few commentaries for various suggestions as to what this might be.

6. The darkening of the sun, moon, and stars may be something entirely beyond our imagination. However, can you think of any ways in which this could happen?

7. What can you find out about the level of geological disturbances and the probability of earthquake activity in the future?

8. Read ecological books such as *Population Bomb, Famine 1975, The Environmental Handbook,* noting how many points tie in with Christ's words.

9. How can Matt 24:34 be understood if it did not apply to the generation which heard Jesus speak?

10. Note especially Luke 21:20-24. Draw up an outline of events in the city of Jerusalem during this present century.